W9-BXW-183

RUNES

A Review of Poetry

signals

CB Follett and Susan Terris, Editors

WINTER SOLSTICE 2005

ARCTOS PRESS

RUNES, A Review of Poetry: Signals

Copyright © 2005 by CB Follett & Susan Terris

All rights reserved. No part of this book may be reproduced or transmitted in any form or by any means, electronic or mechanical, including photocopying, recording or by an information storage and retrieval system without written permission from the editors, individual authors or artists, except for the inclusion of brief quotations in a review.

ISBN 0-9725374-5-3
Library of Congress Control Number 2005906958
Library of Congress Cataloging in Publication Data
1. Poetry 2. Poetry on Signals   3. Poetry -- 21st Century

Book design by Jeremy Thornton, Jeremy Thornton Design

Front cover painting *Les Amants* (1928), René Magritte, National Gallery of Australia, Canberra © 2005 C. Herscovici, Brussels / Artists Rights Society (ARS), New York
Back cover art © by Jeremy Thornton
Inside artwork © by: Diane Rosenblum Althoff, CB Follett, Gertrudis Jarrett, Ann and Dick O'Hanlon (O'Hanlon Center for the Arts, www.ohanloncenter.org), Carolyn Planakis, Marylyn and Jeremy Thornton

Special thanks to Duff Axsom, Gaby Rilleau, Amber Flora Thomas, Joe Zacardi, Sophie Orgish, and Jake Orgish for volunteering time and energy to help us get RUNES out to our contributors and our subscribers.

ARCTOS PRESS
P.O. Box 401
Sausalito, CA 94966-0401
CB Follett: Publisher
Runes, A Review of Poetry e-mail: RunesRev@aol.com
http://members.aol.com/runes

Published and printed in the United States of America on recycled paper.

Call me RUNES, A REVIEW OF POETRY

It is an ancient **RUNES**,
And it stoppeth one of three.

Little **RUNES**, who made thee?

A child said, What is **RUNES**? fetching it to me with full hands;
How could I answer the child? I do not know what it is any more than he.

Buck Mulligan came from the stairhead, bearing a copy of **RUNES** on which a
mirror and a razor lay crossed.

If **RUNES** be the food of love, read on.

Whan that Aprille with its shoures soote,
The wit of **RUNES** hath perced to the roote....

"Christmas wouldn't be Christmas without **RUNES**," grumbled Jo lying on
the rug.

Bright **RUNES**, would I were stedfast as thou art—
Not in lone splendor hung aloft the night....

Listen my children and you shall hear
Of the **RUNES**: Signals of the '05 year.

Many years later as he faced the firing squad, Colonel Aureliano Buendia
was to remember that distant afternoon when his father took him to discover
RUNES.

My heart leaps upwhen I behold
   A **RUNES** upon the shelf.

Whose **RUNES** these are I think I know...

Have we got your attention yet? *Moby Dick; The Rime of the Ancient Mariner;
The Lamb; A Song of Myself; Ulysses; As You Like It; The Canterbury Tales;
Little Women; Bright Star, Would I Were Stedfast as Thou Art; Paul Revere's
Ride; One Hundred Years of Solitude, My Heart Leaps Up When I Behold;
Stopping by Woods on a Snowy Evening.* (If you need to know who wrote each
of these works, ask someone who's currently enrolled in English 101.)

Each year we publish **RUNES, A Review of Poetry** it gets harder to write the opening essay. What can we possibly say now that we haven't said in previous years? But... **RUNES** is still flying high, receiving much critical praise for the excellence of its poetry and for the beauty of its design done, for the fifth time, by the very talented Jeremy Thornton.

This year again, we had more than seven thousand poems from which to choose. "Signals" like "Storm" from last year was for many a hard theme. We didn't want an issue all about traffic lights and racing flags. We looked for interesting angles, poems that felt fresh and original. Because we only select one hundred poems per issue, we turned down hundreds of poems we felt strongly about. Then we wrote notes to each poet saying how hard it is to make these choices.

Poems we fell in love with include pieces about the Underground Railroad, Philip Lamantia, the Igbo, and Montecore – a tiger. We selected poems about Iraq and Armenia, about Ghandi's funeral and child abuse. But we have, as always, poems of nature (look out for wild turkeys and moose) and of the nature of love. Many of the signals in this publication are the subtle signals that go back and forth from one person to another. There are some laugh-aloud poems, too: "A Distant Sunder" by David Alpaugh, "Cheeky" by David Kirby, and "Road Service" by Matt Morris. There's even a literary peeing poem (an oxymoron?); but you'll have to find that one for yourself. There are also poems, we hope, that will make your heart beat faster, ones that may bring tears to your eyes. In short: a varied series of signals, including a few mixed messages.

Our spouses – who look at us each reading every submitted poem at least twice, writing personal notes to all poets who include the requested SASE – say we are eighteenth century women living in a twenty-first century world. One of our loyal subscribers has called us "Godmothers of Poetry." The truth is: we like thinking of ourselves as godmothers and don't mind being, in some way, as thorough and literary as eighteenth century poets and editors. Yes, we'd enjoy a free-wheeling evening of dinner and conversation with Alexander Pope, Jonathan Swift, Robert Burns, and William Blake.

Following along with the theme of eighteenth century rationalism, we'll give you the statistics for this year. **RUNES: Signals** includes forty poets we've published before and sixty poets new to this publication. Fifty-seven of the poets we're publishing here we have never met. Another fifteen or so are poets we may have met once at AWP or some other literary event but still are poets we don't know personally. Of the poems, forty-four are by men and fifty-six by women. There are five translations, including an Aztec song translated by Peter Everwine from the Nahuatl. Five poets in this volume live abroad. Thirty-one different states are represented here plus the District of Columbia. California, New York, and Pennsylvania – three of our most populous states – have the most poets represented.

In the last five years, we have published over four hundred different poets. We consider each of them part of our ever-expanding **RUNES** family. We love to hear about their new awards and publications. One of the highlights of our year was finding out that a poem we'd published by Jane Hirshfield has been chosen for Best American Poetry. But, in one way or another, we consider each of the poems we choose to publish a winner, a star!

Now, it's high time to turn your attention to the stars of this publication: the poems themselves. You'll find pieces by well-known poets such as Shirley Kaufman, W. S. Merwin, Brenda Hillman, Eleanor Wilner, David St. John, and Philip Levine. You'll also meet many poets along the way whose work you've never read. Savor these, too. As in prior years, we tried to weave our hundred poems into some kind of coherent narrative. So start with the poems by Julia Connor (1), Pattiann Rogers (2), and Clifford Browder (3) and read through to ones by Fredrick Zydek (98), Elizabeth Rees (99), and Wendy Mnookin (100). Be sure to pause and appreciate the prize-winning **RUNES Award** poem "Women and Birds" by Sandra Cohen Margulius of Wisconsin and the Runner Up poems by J. O'Nym of Texas and Annalynn Hammond of Wisconsin.

We're process people – so, yes... picture us as you enter the world of **RUNES '05**, standing here in our Godmother guises, waving our wands and beaming at all who would write wonderful poems and those who choose to read them. Now, with abject apologies to T. S. Eliot and other writers whose names we've taken in vain:

Let us go then, you and we,
When the **RUNES** is spread out against the sea
Like....

CB ('Lyn) Follett & Susan Terris, (patient, etherized) editors

TABLE OF CONTENTS

∼

∼

Artwork

≈

signals

m(other) tongue

before...

        when moon and stone
           were the bulwark
      against which   everything pushed
           and blood
               the first syllable
     in the body's cup

      when the pulse
           at the base of the spine
               was a seahorse
           galloping

      before Raven
           tore open history's bag
   or the equines rode
           the rock face of Lascaux

     when *time was the mind of the stars*
              as Pythagoras says
   and the bright arms of motion
         our first song

Lightning from Lightning, I Said

Slice an apple. The instant the blade
pierces the russet-red skin, the knife
is knocked from my hand by the whip
of light let loose. Pluck a blackberry
off the vine and a bolt shoots out
like a needle of neon.

Rays explode outward in all directions
with each step the cougar takes crossing
the rocky hills. (I hear the distant
warning of thunder following.) The scree
of the white-winged hawk is a streak
of fire cutting through the heavens,
splitting them brilliantly, blindingly.
Likewise, fragments of shell left
at the nest reveal the jagged marks
of lightning at work in the hatching.

Similar to the sky, the desert at night
is lit with small fires too. Sizzling
spears of light burst forth as each new
bristle of cactus pushes from its sheaf.
And many of us have seen the series of blue
electric bolts cracking hard, a cavalcade
of shocks, as a glacier breaks, calves,
crashes into the surging bay.

Cataclysms and upheavals are approaching
from everywhere. Think of lightning
in the thought of lightning. Even by
nodding our heads now, the "amen"
almost spoken, a blazing potential
is gathering, building, poised to strike.

There is an untapped power of light
lying dormant in each crystal grasp
in every splinter of snow falling tonight
over the icy valleys of the Himalayas.

A Wasp Smothered in Marmalade

A wasp smothered in marmalade
Lily rot
Bat clusters, sticky buds

Ashtrays in cancer wards, cushioned caskets

Through archipelagoes of night
Islands of dream

Two rattlesnakes vertically entwined
Dancing snails
Hoots of ghostly owls:

Signals I must heed, decipher.
Who sends them? Why?
What mysteries beckon?
What dangers loom?

All day
I am beset with signals:
Scissors that won't cut
Telephone shrieks
Lost files
A matchbook cover: LOVE

This computer has performed
An illegal operation
And will be shut down

From the street below
Rumbles, ratatats.

Signals
Entice, unsettle me:
Finger-thick worms
Green cheese
A wound's yellow juices

Star rubble
Moans from the abyss
Roiling
My bone once the stuff of galaxies
My blood the sea.

Who Is Federico?

He plays the strings
of the white chair like a lute,

drums his fingers on the water pipes.
I hear rain on the skylight.

His voice coming over the answering machine
sings to me in long, blue shadows,

like the white road the moon casts on the sea.
Who is Federico?

His big fish feet can't fit
into his funny shoes.

He leaves messages – jumbled footprints in mud
wildly dancing in my driveway,

serenades me with jungle rhythms on the doorbell,
then runs away like a kid on Halloween.

Notes to me pinned on trees, bleached out by the sun,
or blurred with rain. Who is Federico?

If anybody knows, tell him this has been a long courtship.
Tell him I am growing old. Tell him: have courage.

Tell him, like Dorothy Parker,
I never liked a man I didn't meet.

Your Fate

Waiting for the tech support person
to come back, re-reading the epic –
actually, the translator's notes; strange to
start liking the on-hold music (Here's
a section where chaotic motion, interims
of wandering, invisible orders meet twisted
blue marginalia from school, doodles, what
wasn't done behind a page giving
way to cricket operas – ch-chch – &
eucalyptus residue under various protests in
spring; you could find a golden
twig, go sexily to hell, play
music below; some epics are interchangeable;
others agree to the maenads, not
you; a Sybil sings in smoggy
crags behind the hill; harps might
help, units of twelve; chance rides
at your back on his bike
but fate rides only in reverse)
tech support hasn't returned yet but
he will (there's a patient tap-
tap tapping in the text; an
inviolable tree where stars pass;
stars passed; stars pierced you –

Of the owl: stripped of

Of the owl: stripped of its feathers, the naked
bird would weigh less than
its feathers, owls are all wings, are all feathers,
weigh nearly nothing

this is an owl feather,

already important to her. She has it wrapped in
a bit of cloth in her purse. She believes in bird
magic. It's watching her. Her tired coal-rimmed
eyes, black suns leveled in them, watch back.

In this, there may be no

bodies but the land. How mountain spills his
seed to a sea. How a blue heron
perches at its wet circumference of dawn.
How a field only wants to be
bedded, the spotted owl to circle it
and circle it because dusk is
its dinner hour, moonlight its house.

In this, we are not

skin and we have no story. If we devour
one another, it is as the elements
feed on us, outlast us. In this, there is
fire and water, air and earth, and no fear.
Is love necessary in this?

At the horizon

where mushroom and orange fungus and
bark and moist and twitter
hush, and are one. On the river, dragonflies
born. One garden that was never planted.
Skin that was never used or shed. Cells
metastasizing like music when music has
never been. How the mountain lifts, and
spills his seed. How the sea is the sea
and a cannibal feeds upon herself, before growing old.

Cococuicatl

Toco toco tiquiti tocon tiquitin toco toco tiquiti
Nompehua yaho nicuicanitl nõnitotia nitozquatectzin ayao
Nicnotlanehuia nocuic noxochiuh ayoppã tlalticpac
      niquihtohuaya nitozquatectzin ayao
Çan no niaz ayao ohuaye yca nichocaya a yhua niyahuia
      nocuic noxochiuh haa
Nicuicanitlan a nixochipapalotl aya ninochiuhtiaz teixpana nipatlãtiaz
      ayyahue a yhuan niyahuia nocuic noxochiuh haa

Onca yahue aya nepapan tototl moyahuatimani ylhuicaatl ymanca
   yectli y atl a ytempa aya oncan niehua noca yehua notayohuã
   ma xiyahui mochan a ompa ye cuextlan ho hanca yahue
Çan ca ye nocuic onca yahue haya cacalotla yehuaya niquehuaco ye
   nican cilin ihcahuacaya teucciztli y tzatziya oncan niyehua moca
   ichua nottayohuan ma xiyahuiyan mochã ompa ye cuextlã
   o hanca y Et.

TRANSLATOR'S NOTE:

This poem was adapted from the Nahuatl (language of the Aztecs) using the text of *Cantares Mexicanos* (as alphabetized by the early Spanish Friars). "Cococuicatl" means "dove song" but I've changed the title to conform to the singer's announcement. The first line after the title refers to the drum rhythm used with this song. I've not included that or any of the purely rhythmic vocables indicated in the text.

Cuextlan was on the Gulf Coast, east from the Mexican highland and thus in the direction of the rising sun (the Aztec national deity was a war/solar god). The poem belongs to a type of song quest. In some ways, the maker of this poem seems to be a sort of Aztec Wallace Stevens.
– P.E.

The Song of Parrot-Crest Lord

Now I begin to sing,
I'm Parrot-Crest Lord, and I dance.
I borrow, for a time, my songs and flowers.
One day I must return them –
And so I lament
And take pleasure in songs and flowers.

I'm the singer:
I'll turn into flower butterfly.
At the side of others I'll take flight
And look for pleasure in songs and flowers.

Where the sky whirls in a tumult of birds,
Where the sea stretches far away,
By the shore of the good water –
I'm going there...
                          Be with me, fathers,
To your home in Cuextlan!
Only in the country of ravens
Will I find my songs
And return to sing them.

Where conch shells roar and the horns call out
I'm going there...
                          Be with me, fathers,
To your home in Cuextlan!

It was the day she stumbled upon a flock of wild turkeys

and they all flew up and away
except one tom who faced her
and fanned his tail feathers out like a poker hand.
It was the same day she found a sparrow's nest
blown from a yew tree by the wind
and made entirely of her own hair.
It was the day things turned for the better,
always she would see that day as
her very own dove holding green in its beak,
showing that the rain was done,
that there was dry land
somewhere.

Now – You Also, Sparrow

Seven leaves left on the sweetgum and one flock
       of drab finches – eleven, twelve birds? As crows,
   this would signal something: false riches, or the brazen thievery
of time. As finches, they stand only for what they are:
       quick eyes, hollow bones, the restless hunger
       of even the smallest lives. Watch how they tilt
their attention to the wind, intent on its lush pronunciations
of *SOUTH*. One strong gust and they'll depart, at once, together:
       yellow gloried from the tree
          in every winged direction. Of course,
we always knew it would come to this. Of course, we alone
feel emptied. The barren branches, or the branches, laden,
       do not falter from their spiral trance.

Still Life

Plum

In the corner, just dark enough
to seem sinister, yet one curve
lit, a brilliant purple bruise. This plum
remembers sunlight, but if you pressed
your thumb firmly against its skin,
its flesh would split open soft
as a fish's slit belly. What do you think
would crawl out? Shiny red ants,
or perhaps a lizard's tongue,
a few grains of sand – remember,
this plum knew sunlight once.

Glass Vase with Painted Blue Wing

The wing, of course, is to represent time,
its passing. The vase is empty, clear,
and the plum's shadow encroaches behind it.
The space that is unfilled inside this vase
is there for a reason, but the reason is unknown
to anyone except the blue wing, who, like time,
doesn't speak. Nothing belongs
in the vase because it's like your throat
right before it wants to sing, but doesn't.

Nickel

A simple token, a familiar face.
(The nickel is far from the plum's shadow
and to the right of the vase. It has the effect
of drawing your eye away for a second,
and then, only being flat and silver,
it sends your eye back.)

Black Silk Stocking

Stretched in front of the vase,
its toe brushing the rim of the nickel,
probably to make you uncomfortable.
It's evidence of something that took place
before, maybe even under the one
watchful eye of the plum. Whatever it was,
you can be sure it wasn't pleasant,
for the one-legged thing
that must've been involved
crawled away, out of its skin.

Gray Walnut in Shell

> At the open wound end
> of the silk stocking, in the shadow
> of the plum, to the left
> of the vase, far from the nickel
> (its evil twin). I don't know why
> there always must be a walnut,
> but at the least we can infer
> it is supposed to allude to the pit
> inside the plum (which unlike
> the plum's flesh, has never known sunlight
> and will not until eaten), and also,
> being hard and tight as a skull
> plastered with clay, it's about
> the fear of our own tombs.

Photograph

> Flat on the table, in front
> of the silk stocking and the vase,
> between the nickel and the walnut,
> exactly one foot from the plum.
> This photo cannot be seen
> unless you are in the room
> and are most likely the artist.
> But I have it on good faith
> this photo is of a small girl,
> no more than five, with dirt

on her face and black silk stockings
under her blue dress. I've also been told
this photo was taken directly after
the girl, while reaching for a plum
in the top cupboard, knocked
her mother's favorite glass vase
to the floor. She then gave her brother,
who saw everything, a nickel
not to tell, and ran outside
under the black walnut tree.
He must not have told, for her mother
came outside later and took her picture,
saying she'd seen her from the window,
staring at one gray walnut between her fingers,
and it was a haunting image, to see a child
so lost in simple things.

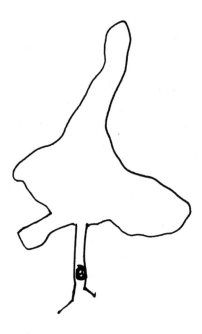

It looked much better than this. Some artist drew it
the way they do with lines which are never straight
and curves that have something else in them like
breath, or some inscrutable motion.
On a cement wall it was yellow for the trunk,
green for the canopy and even a brown knot
whirling in a lovely way which seemed without
effort. Beneath this tree was one word, stamped,
not written, in black: **PLANT**.
I drew up close thinking it was a definition,
only to realize it was not that at all –
it was a command. Plant! Go plant! An exhortation
to the world. To all who are green. To all
who are not green. To me.
I smiled the whole day
filling the earth with forests.

The Leaf

There is the girl, with one leg swung over the porch rail,
the other small foot wedged between the railings, squared thick
like the trunk of her old wood doll –
she is drawn by the light and the lack of it,
by the face of a green leaf at the edge of the woods,
and all the other faces,
she is drawn to it as though gathered to it,
as though the light gathers her up and paints a bright spot –
she is a child, her darkness is at the edge of the woods,
her darkness is her sadness and her grief
but not only, it is the world,
and the way it speaks to her,
and the way the world is the lack of the world,
and all is in a bright spot and a shadow behind it,
and the birch tree, and the broken arm of the old elm,
and the wings of a common gull as it brushes
down to the water,
all speak of it.

House of Paper

On a balcony, a girl lights a lantern.
Paper unpleats into a cylinder of light.
She sways her arm to anticipate the wind.
She knows happiness is a flame
rising straight in a house of paper.

In a house of paper, the walls are lined
with festive tales of the moon, from mother
to daughter, each year, mid-autumn:
an empress once stole an elixir from
her husband. Some say she was greedy;
others, that she saved the people
from her tyrant husband, his thirst
for immortality. She swallowed,
and drifted into the sky. She lives yet,
a goddess in exile on the moon.
By her side, a woodcutter chops
a self-healing tree, and a rabbit grinds
herbs with mortar and patient pestle.

The girl knows while the night-blooming
cereus unfolds, they will only whisper.
It is safe to light candles. Tomorrow,
when voices quarrel, she will hide
on the moon, in a house of paper.

Her father presses a dull-edged knife
into a mooncake. They each hold
a piece, careful not to crumble
the dry yolk rounded by sky-dark paste,
salt and sugar in equal measure.

In a park below, a boy draws luminous
orbits with the tip of a branch, the last embers
of a bonfire. The girl asks for one more
story. Her mother tells her to look

in the sky. The moon is brimming,
as if to overflow into tomorrow.

Shame

When my five-year-old, not listening, climbed over
        the broken fence head first

and fell (the gash on his cheek, a huge backward "C"),
        we didn't recognize, as he bled,

what he'd opened up for himself
        until the next morning at dawn

when he ghost-walked into my room
        as was his custom (to lie with me

or wake me) – only this time he stood himself
        face into the corner, face to the wall,

and said, *I don't want you to look at it.*
        Only my story – which his wound opened

up for me – seemed to comfort him:
        as though imagining his mother as a

six-year-old, nose-to-nose with a collie,
      while her friend, unbeknown to her,

pulled his tail while saying *Kiss Brandy*, though
      the dog lunged before I could

and fanged my upper lip and cheek, my son
      cheek-to-cheek with me

could hold his story up with mine and bear
      the shame of the gash, the stitches

or the fear of them, the stinging dab of ointment,
      the questions always asked that are

another gash – the one that never heals, that re-opens
      and bleeds when asked.

Prepubescence

He was six when in the office he colored this big black keyhole on a
blue Post-It and stuck it to the edge of a shelf. It's like a cartoon door
on a dungeon without walls or windows. Sometimes I've moved it,
unconsciously, hunting a book, yet a hundred times stood before a
thing so stark it seemed there before he made it, what only a child
could see to create, a reminder he can't be reminded of it, that for now
there's no escape.

Boys

They jiggle it, fidget it,
Twist it, poke it,
Pound it, beat time on it,
Stomp all over it;

They can turn up the volume on even a book –
Spine goes squack
Pages flabble flabble flabble

If it won't at least chirp
When you smack it on the head
You can never be quite sure about it:

Boys, banging on the world, make it sing.

A Distant Sunder

What God hath joined together,
let not man put—

I used to solder.
The reasons why are now obscure.
Maybe just to bring old junk back to life:
a clock, a ceiling fan, my father's Philco;
to see or hear gizmos, gone silent or dark,
whirr,
light up, or sound an alarm.

There was a rude art to it, and an odor:
the shock of a barely audible *pfusssst;*
a sudden melt; quick hardening.

Just a lad, fooling around in dad's cellar;
making intimate connections;
bringing strands of copper
– cleansed of dirt & grease –
together (or back together)
with a silvery ring.

> *Do you, wire, A, take this wire, C,*
> *to be your lawful wedded weld?*

As I built each bridge over troubled metal,
pulses quickened; couples thrummed: *I do!*

But Judas snuck into my make-believe chapel
and hid in the last pew; while the parson
argued a slam-dunk case against betrayal.

Still, I heard God's demiurge say:
> *Do what fasteners may,*
> *love & solder will be kissed away*
> *by a distant sunder.*

Sleight of Hand

Boys in high school hurt so bad,
they said, *You're giving me blue balls,*
that's how much they wanted to touch you.
After a while, you took pity, couldn't stand
being called tease or you liked the boy.
You'd find him beneath white cotton
with hands somehow twice normal size,
ready to enter new terrain, *Just for a minute, baby,*
as though fingers had clocks, tick-ticking away,
impossible to believe at that moment a boy's hands
had only twenty-seven bones and sixty muscles,
same as a girl's.

In the locker room, Miss Hildebrand warned us
about Roman hands and Russian fingers,
but no one paid attention, mesmerized
by the movement under a pristine bra, while
you pretended you didn't know it was there –
the touch that turned you from good girl
to bad so fast you figured, why not everything?
The way Lewis and Clark must have felt,
arriving at the Mississippi: If we cross this divide,
we might as well go on to the end.
They waved, hands beckoning,
urging the others to take a chance.

Skipping Stones

He could displace the face of any lake,
barely break the surface, convince the water
to kiss the rock, convince the rock to resist.

He'd search cracked shale beds baking in the sun,
culling hydrodynamic from asymmetric,
the millions of stones from the millions of years

lying smoothed and wind-brushed in the hush of noon.
And yes there was passion in the way he caressed
his perfect decision, sucked a finger to test the breeze,

then skimmed light with just the right english
to skip it eight, ten, a dozen times before it sank
as I watched the concentric circles of ripples

intersect from each step the stone had taken
to form a secret map of the world
that nobody knows how to read.

Requiem for Judith Clare

1.

The years she came to me,
three-year-old of the blond hair and wide eyes,
spirit by the side of the bed, the girl-child
who drowned with her father, my uncle, in the lake outside town.

Ghost angel. How long I could lie there, unmoving,
my body frozen under the tower
of her gaze. Like a diver
deep underwater, shadowed by the keel, the boat
drifting and bobbing in the glare overhead.

Looking and being looked at. Seeing and being seen.
Unseeing and unseen all the same.

Center of centers, seed of seeds,
almond wrapped up in sweetening itself.

Until – like a double vision, no longer blurring – suddenly single –
like a movie screen going bright in a dark theater –
a window shade, or the iris of a camera, thrown open –

pupil and retina, eyelid and eye would explode.

2.

Then, like a swimmer breaking the surface, lungs
bursting for breath,
I would bolt from bed, race out of the room,
turning on lights at each doorway I passed
till I finally fled
out of the house into the night, the door locked,
body shaking with cold.

Thirty minutes,
forty miles south of town,
two in the morning at a friend's front door,
knocking and waking her from sleep,
afraid to talk and asking to stay until just before dawn
when I rose, wrote a note, drove home.

All these things, including all of the stars.
Blessed be the flower of your death.

Little one, you have swum underwater all my life.

3.

Dreams, recollections, memories. Changing shape,
trading places and names.

I remembered I'd seen her,
the two of us children together, a boy and girl,
two maybe three years old,
attending her father's, my uncle's, wake.

(*Wake.* As if a death were a sleep. As if the old round
were telling the truth. A rowboat,
a tune on a bright stream.)

A tomboy, she'd raced up to me, lacquer black shoes,
sliding across the hardwood floor,
taking my hand to give me a shove, sending me
sprawling down the steps.

(Only *that*, her sister, my cousin
explained, at a funeral or wedding, twenty years later –
that wasn't possible.)

Yes, her father, my uncle, was one of the bodies
laid out at the house on Circular Street,
the polished black enamel
of a coffin crossways under the arch to the back room.

Uncle Paul.

See, you feel as if you've let everything go.

But the second coffin, smaller, holding the daughter –
that was Judith, Judith Clare.

For you are contained in what does not end
and there the strong tides ebb and flow.

Her older sister, catching her breath, telling me this,
sister who married,
bore a daughter,
naming the girl for the drowned sister.

4.

Dreams, memories, recollections –

and my cousin comes no more, visitor
watching from the gown of her silence, weaving

my nights like a wraith, a saint of lost childhood,
emptying the house of my dreams.

For you are contained in what does not end,
and there the strong waves rise and fall.

The gain and loss, the riddle in this.
Unseen and seen all the same.

5.

She is gone, the young girl, Judith Clare, my cousin.
Gone as her father before her.

No visits now.

Only by the water, after a wave breaks and retreats,
slips and slows and slides
down the sand, do I hear – not a voice –
more a whisper,
like a voice overheard, a rustling of leaves
or the give and take of the reeds
that root and stand at the edge of the marsh –

as if the shore or the water were breathing,
remembering to breathe,
learning or remembering what language is for,
how once it was to talk.

For it's already begun in you,
what will burn beyond the suns.

6.

These lines are water, Judith Clare,
weaving the English with words from the German
the poet your father would have known,

writing of the Buddha enlightened,
the seer in glory,

water for the child who was and is no longer
and will always be there.

The Sap of Spring

He lit the buds just forming on the branch-tips,
lit them like candles. The sap of spring
sizzled at the kiss of the match, sputtering,
a tree of buds that would not be candles, as if
his birthday wasn't enough, as if the sky –
nice rich blue – was a blowing wind
that snuffed candles for a living – nice tree,

its bark a ruffled pelt, skin outside skin,
like the summer tan that sloughs off in long
mica-ed sheets. We used to sit at the end
of the dock and peel the boys –
long, curling patches of them –
want to keep them in scrapbooks, but they
were only the stuff of boys who smelled of salt
and hidden cigarettes.

We left their backs tattered like the pinto ponies
we rode on Wednesdays, aiming them
toward the low white fences, hoping
when they jumped they would use
their own good sense and not rely on
messages from our legs – nice ponies
with their mud-caked hoofs
we patent-leather-shined for gymkhanas,
reins loose on their necks, our nice
taut rumps tucked into English saddles,

rounding on the canter – nice leather smell,
rising like tree-sap under us – leather
and some primal woman-smell beginning,
nice smell, the boys thought
sneaking a sniff of saddles in the tack room
the way they used to smell our bicycle seats,
some aphrodisiac they would grow into,
boys with hot eyes that wanted things,
that talked about the things they wanted,
with a can of Schlitz and a Camel, things
they wanted but didn't yet know how to get –
the promise of nice things,

and the ponies, turned out to graze, nibbled
with their fat square teeth,
their nice muzzles soft against the hand
offering carrot, sugar cube,
their brown eyes half-lidded,
right legs cocked – shapely legs –
better than Nancy Betrow's, whose legs
could do things to boys – nice boys –
but vulnerable as wheat before the reaper.

The little ponies with their yellow/green teeth,
and their whisk-tails chasing off flies,
brushed our faces, necks, shoulders,
teeth nuzzling, tails whispering –
nice tails – nice ponies.

With a tip of the hat to Gerald Stern

Invitation

Under trees I begin to row.
Rings rock and fold into silence behind me.
Moss drips from high branches. Full moon.
Already the tree frogs trill up the evening.
Owl's asleep. Insects whine.

I pole into the swamp, back to the dark
of childhood, back to the ocean where
the first boy kissed me and lights glittered
in the distance. I pole among roots, back
to the sulfur pool where I floated

with my first man-love in pungent steam.
I pole among solemn trunks.
These are my women.
Their under-garments are dark, wet
circles where water sank during the night.

I've made a pouch of knots, a white net
to hunt eel. My moon has come. I am old enough
to make my way. Everywhere
the frogs are deafening.
The boat inches forward, wobbles

and bumps. One of mine raises her knee
just under the sepia surface. I am stopped.
The gray bent leg is firm. So here
in the moon's half-light I lower the net,
virgin in brackish water. I move with it

under, between the generous legs of my people.
Slow white slithering. *Come eel. Find me*, I call.
I am wet. I'm here in the water. Listen,
I am movement. I am the vibrating frog,
the owl's opening eye. I am the whole night.

Commencement

School's last day you slip in, let my office door
slide shut, to offer up wild strawberries . . .
and something new – pollen on the wind?
a musk? bright lips, that were plain,
a row of earrings replacing the single pearl?

You study my face instead of the floor,
listen and smile with an unhurried secret –
one who knows she's present and future,
come to say goodbye with a lingering hug.
My arm around your sunburnt shoulders –
how else to do it?
                    Now *I'm* shy of words
to say this: you're an explosion on an atoll –
its palm fringe, its necklace of sand, blue
to the horizon – a commotion climbing fast.
I'd forgotten how it is to wake into a self
with a body.
                    Some combust in a delicate
puff, some in a shower of sparks – but you
in a great column headed up, propelled by
a heat that ignites what you touch and what
stands near. Even now you're close enough
to warm my face; I laugh to stir the breeze.

Don't misunderstand: I'm dizzy in your
more-than-natural light – it gives every
plane a sharper edge – and my days are less
serene than you believe. But I feel another –
a downward – tug: blown west on the trades,
others I love are winking out on every side,
ash on my shoulders.

                So this is where
our vectors cross, a breathless X. Oh you
could buoy me aloft awhile and I could
freight you with ballast enough. But I can't
climb your warm updraft and you shouldn't
cool too soon.
             Still, this sudden turbulence
as we eddy in each other's wake – it's
in your eyes, a deep expectant dare
that startles me with what's left unsaid.

Independence Day

The man in front of me at the fireworks
is rubbing his hands on his girlfriend's back
like he's washing a window. Now that's
no way to treat a dirty girl! I'll bet
he's a big cat, too, when he's kissing her,
sticking his tongue out, all spit and polish,
like he's licking a boot in some army,
like he's scouring a cone for the last bit
of butter pecan. The girlfriend lingers
her fingers along her brow, so slow
I'm mesmerized, a subtle semaphore –
the way you'd dab at your own lips, or wipe
your own nose, tipping your oblivious friend
to his mustard moustache or his smuts – but
this bozo just scrubs harder. As fireworks
fizzle out there in the night, I watch her
flick her tongue to her own ticklish wrist, like
she's savoring for herself her own
sweet and sour, her own vinegar and salt.

Travelers

Creamy afternoon light in old Santa Barbara.
Drifting cigarette smoke in Aix en Provence.
The sheer humid weight of the Yucatan.
You can only be where you are.

But the couple already accept this:
he has a nose like a wolf and a pigeon's homing compass;
she can sense a temperature shift of one degree –
there can never be enough blankets.

Picture two travelers in a hotel bed,
mattress sloping to the middle like a glacial Swiss valley
and all night long they've been boulders colliding.
Backs aching, they dress to sip green breakfast tea.

He says: "I found a dead spider in the dresser drawer,
all eight legs pointed as black knitting needles,
upside down and the circumference of a shitake.
It looked like it had been there a long time."

She says: "They have no words for 'good luck'.
What they say is 'much rain.'"
He says: "Do you smell something burning?"
She says: "Is it cold in here?"

The waitress comes and takes their order.
He aligns knives, folds the *International Herald*.
She studies maps, rates of exchange, their tabletop world
round and flat, with edges to fall off in every direction.

Cheeky

I say, "I'm looking for a book by Apuleius,"
      and the girl says, "First name?" and I say,
  "He had only the one," and she says, "Title?"
and I say, "Um, *The Golden Ass!*" and she says,
  "I have one of those!"– not, I think, meaning to be
      flirty with your present hero but merely practicing
the famed English bluntness which contrasts so vividly

with the famed English politesse, and here I think
      of the beggar who asks for spare change, and I fumble
  with my coins and finally say, "Here, take it all,"
and he replies, "Are you sure?" and when I say, well,
  I *was* thinking of buying a newspaper, he counts out
      35 pence and hands them back as passersby scowl
at this ragged fellow placing a stack of copper

in the palm of my well-dressed self. And – oh, ha! –
      how funny it would have been had the young woman
  in the bookstore made a punning reference to
Sir Francis Drake's *Golden Hinde*, a replica of which
  is moored nearby on the Thames and whose figurehead
      is the noggin of a smiling ungulate, not some
cheeky shop girl's gilded tushy! On the same river

is anchored a ship on which Barbara and I saw a production
        of *Othello* one night, and I hope you appreciate
    that I said "anchored," reader, because – oh, ha, ha! –
I almost said "moored" again! For what a course
    is this English of ours, so rich from its Latin
            and Germanic tributaries that it floods the land
with jokes, puns, wisecracks, bagatelles, banterings, and drolleries

of every sort as well as double entendres. I wonder if the young lady
        in the bookstore had heard the one about the guy
    who decided he wanted to write a letter,
so he asks the shop girl if she keeps stationery,
    and she blushes and says, "Well, I try, but sometimes
            I wriggle around a bit towards the end." Well, if not,
I wasn't going to be the one to tell her! Though her being

English and Shakespeare being Shakespeare,
            i.e., as omnipresent in the culture as beans on toast
    and tube strikes, I'm sure she's familiar with the scene
in *Twelfth Night* where Malvolio finds the fake note
    from Olivia and says, "By my life, this is my lady's hand:
            these be her very C's, her U's, and her T's;
and thus she makes her great P's." Spinoza says the wish

of all things is to continue to be what they are:
         the stone wishes to be stone, the tiger, tiger, and so on.
   Not so people, I think. Cities, yes, but not people.
Take Westminster, for example – it's the tony part
   of the city now because it was then, for prevailing winds
         usually blow from the west, so that if you arrive early
and dig in, the winds will blow to the east

the odors not only of your personal whiffs, poots,
         farts, barfs, teetees, weewees, busters, whizzes,
   bunts, B.O.s, eructations, extrusions, cigar fumes,
cooking fires, and chemical experiments gone wrong
   but also those of your associates, kinsmen,
         and livestock. Not so much your person, though,
for example, your Lucius, hero of *The Golden Ass*

and one who, near the end of the many adventures
         that befell him after turning into a donkey as the result
   of a magic spell gone wrong, likened himself
to Ulysses, "a wise man who had traveled
   divers countries and nations, and by straitly observing
         them all had obtained great virtue and knowledge,"
wherefore this Lucius says, "I do now

give great thanks to my assy form,"
for "I have seen the experience of many things,
and am become more experienced (notwithstanding
that I was then very little wise)." Well – all right!
Paul Revere didn't say, "The British are coming!"
but something along the lines of "The people
who are going to remain British are coming, ·

so those of us who are about to become Columbians
or Washingtonians or whatever, best prepare
to resist them vigorously!" And so we did,
and so we've earned the right to wear t-shirts
saying "I Used to Think Americans Were Stupid
and Now I Are One" and to be thankful
for those parts of our bodies our mommies swatted

as well as praised and that serve us so well today
as seats, fashion accessories, objects to be patted,
kissed, scratched, squeezed, and whistled at,
sources of jokes and insults, conduits of all
that is earthy in us on its journey back
to the earth so that, each night and then
first thing again every day, we may be angels.

The Beginning of Cubism

1. The painter

He takes her apart. It is April.
That which is vertical, that which has edges,
that which is not recognizable.
A torso is a line. The baby is in the corner.
It has not yet been born.
The way it bends means nothing.
He pulls the shapes from her skin.
This is your heart in the center,
where it tricks the eye into believing
red.

2. The model

She dreams he is touching her,
the way his hand moves up and
down the canvas, the way his stare
breaks her open. She imagines him
gutting a papaya, reaching up inside her,
pulling the seeds out. The way he will devour
her nipples, the tongue kiss of his brush
as he flecks them with pearls, how she will walk
off the canvas, her image burning into
the smaller canvasses of the mind.

In the darkness of sleep, she will ignite
every man's fantasy.
How they will circle around her
wondering what it would be like
to draw the blush from between her legs,
run their fingers along the contour of her hips,
the subtle hunger of her body, the first peach
of summer.

3. The canvas

When she looks at the canvas,
she will not recognize herself,
the way he has cut her up.
They will not understand
that I was beautiful,
she tells him.

When We Want to Disbelieve

How many times has he seen it,
the lonely black of crow
blinking across the sky.

There are times when he regards it
as a rent in the fabric,
a tear in perception,
flapping open and shut,
open and shut.

"Look what comes after.
Look what's beyond your blue sky,
behind your forest landscape:
darkness,
ultimates of space and time,
things you may never know,
things to disprove you."

Like sitting around the living room
during Thanksgiving,
watching the old super eight
strobing on the wall.
All the relatives thoughtfully humming
at the cubs and pups of their youth,
as if to lick the salt of birth off their proper hides.

There, his brother
streaking across the ball field,
running faster than man
and laws of nature.
And he asks,
"How can cancer ever catch that youth?"
but this is
as elusive as crows and rents.

His brother running, ball in hand,
beyond the breadth of super eights.
The crowd, in focus, still looking on
beyond their brilliance on the wall.
The crowd still cheering his brother,
running, somewhere beyond the limits.

Crow, film, Ronnie.
Three things making him disbelieve.

Spell against Depression

*In Gypsy philosophy, depression attracts depression like a vibration. To ward it off,
walk to a hilltop. Look down on roads, cars, houses, people. Place several peeled garlic
cloves in a saucer of white vinegar beside your bed while you sleep. Bury them in the
morning.*

In the months when I lay buried, it was
hard to stay still.
                    At night I awoke
and listened to the sounds of birds
in the eaves or deeper, perhaps,
under the rafters.
                    Often I'd walk about the house in the chill dark,
rearranging the furniture, tilting the photographs in their frames
a fraction of an inch.
                    When daylight came
I'd return to sleep, curled up like a
garlic clove inside the thin sheath of my
skin, keeping the violence of white blossoms,
the murderous light from the hollows of my
body.
                    In the evening, when
it was safe to breathe, I'd walk out
past the city limit sign, into the hills,
the air crowded with the sad inflections
of birds, their piercing notes,
their troubling red wingbeats
lifting, resettling in the no-light,

          and turning round,
I'd see the busy roads, the cars, houses, people,
made small, made nameless.
                    Though I could not disappear
as I wanted, I could, sometimes, ward off
the pain of living, forget heaven, forget
the shriek of the pulley and angels fluttering
like shirts pinned to the line.
Then the darkness, thickening
in the hill's creases.

          Everywhere
the dead are shifting,
making room for the living. They tug
at the corner of our sleep, tug us
awake to the waking world,
                   the room crossed
suddenly with shadow and the wings of birds
no one sees.

Full Hunger Moon

Forty years of hunger. Look:
    her lover is fat, so fat
gorging
    on the pretty stick in the boudoir
trying to keep her make-up straight
    each time he lunges:
I am joyful, my love, he says,
    feeding.
Her eyes: ripped nets.
    Her heart: squashed fruit.
Her breasts are emptied vats
    that knew the moon and other rich phases, once;
oddly quilted commotion
    she feels skinned without.
What is survival
    but a magician's quick mirror, the magician
of second-hand sleeves,
    canned applause.

I am joyful, my love.

      It is not joy that keeps him here,
her needy,

      ravenous plump puppy:
full as a tick, he drops

      off – sobbing.
Famished baby, careless,
carnivorous boy, greedy daddy:

      I can't fill your twisted spoon.

      O my hunger, my hunger...
Swift as a suicide it's finished

      with a groan round as the O in the mute, fat
moon.

      Alone with empty bottles and chicken bones, she
watches

      February's blue dawn test
her painted toes; tonight

      she believes she'll start with

        soup.

The 167th Psalm of Elvis

Blessed are the marble breasts of Venus,
those ancient miracles, for they are upright and milk white
and they point above the heads of the crowd in the casino.
Blessed are the crowds that play, and whose reflections
sway in the polish of her eggshell eyes,
for they move in shimmers and flights of birds
as they circle the games
and they are beautiful and helpless.
Bless the fast glances that handle the waitress,
bless her miniskirt toga and the flame-gold scotch,
and bless the gamblers who gaze at the stage.
Remember also the dancer and remember her dance,
her long neck arched like a wild white goose,
the tassels on her nipples that shoot like sparks,
and bless the legs and bless the breasts
for they are fruit and honey
and they are generous to the eyes.
Have mercy on my wallet, the dollars I punch into the slot,
and grace the wheels swapping clubs and hearts.

Mercy on me too, as I stumble as if in a hashish haze
watching the reels spin away, for I am a blown fuse
and I need someone to bless me before it's too late.
Honor the chance in a million, the slot machine jolting,
the yellow light flashing, honor the voice that calls *jackpot*,
and the coins that crush into the brushed steel tray,
for there is a time for winning and a time for losing
and if you cast your bread upon the waters
you will find it again after many days.
Pity the crowd around the blessed winner
all patting his back as if it rubs off,
this juice, this force, this whatever
that might save them from their own cursed luck.
And pity the poor winner whose hand claws back
into his bucket of coins and who cannot walk away,
because he'd do anything for the feeling
he had when the great pattern rose from the chaos
of cherries and lemons and diamonds and stars
and he knew for that moment he was blessed.

Hamlet as an International Student

When leaving for England and leaving your kingdom to
The care of an absent-minded father and an insatiable mother,
Expecting more money and better times to come,
One must not hope for a quick return.

Blowing away the beer foam, feeling up red-haired bimbos,
Listening to your buddies' deliberations on
The mysterious mentality of the Danes, you're OK, but, hark!
Do not start wondering why everything you once knew had disappeared.

The moment you boarded the ship in the port,
With its cargo of old, smelly herring and heretics on board,
Your previous place became a black hole,
A button that fell off, a wet floor board.

The problem is not that your old blockhead-friends lost their loyalty to you,
Not that your ex-home does not remember you anymore.
Quite to the contrary: it will become a museum soon,
And the new tenant will take his profit there. Drop by drop.

Everything will be like before, only you are shelved.
Our past is like a cat: pet it, give it some food.
If you'll trust it to someone else's care – the vocabulary has gone thinner,
And alien mollusks have stuck themselves to the ship's bottom.

Our past is Diva. Just look away for a second,
Look, she's already offering the bed to a stranger.
When you leave for an island, you'd better forget about the continent.
Forget about your attempts to build a Flying Ark.

T-Bone and Zeus

I.

Zeus will go 'cross the world for a good martini.

Zeus had a Chinese girl at the Berlin Wall
        an Indian girl at the Liberty Bell
        an actress in Vegas.
Started to tell him 'bout this girl I knew named Kea,
Zeus didn't want to hear it.

Zeus shoots his mouth
after too many martinis
punches your shoulder
like he ain't the thunder god.

Zeus and I at this Goth club.
What's a black man suppose to do at a Goth club?
"Naw, Zeus, you need to come down to this place I know.
Dey got a sea of good-hair girls
who'll step on a nigga for a Greek god."
Zeus like, "You for real, T?"
Lift my shirt; show him boot marks.

So Zeus on the dance floor:
somewhere between the Structure jacket
and Bandstand moves
finds the blonde in the room,
buys her a martini.

We're outside
blowing smoke in the cold
here comes Zeus all alone.
We're like "Zeus!
What happen to that girl you talkin' to?"
An' Zeus is like, " We didn't work out.
I turned her into a cow."

We laugh; go for mash potatoes.

II.

My cousin rolls into town
in one of those slick black skirts
that looks good on any girl
that's not your cousin.

My cousin wore this smile
gave her eyes to guys
then she ask them to leave
when they wouldn't leave
she gave her eyes to me
and I
would ask them to leave.

but this is Zeus
and this is my cousin
and this is why they call it drama.

We're at the bar
and my cousin's laughing
and Zeus is smiling
and one leads the other to the dance floor.

Zeus: Zeus is this hand moving up her arm.
               Zeus is this breath blowing in her ear.
               Zeus is this body creeping on her
a cloud creeping on a summer day,
and this is Zeus
but this is my cousin
and this is why they call it drama.

We're leaving the club
in the car
heading to the hotel
and I'm ready
ready for eyes
ready for thunder
ready to throw down 12 rounds
and do this thing
they call drama

and

      nothing.

My cousin out the car
with a "call you tomorrow"
leaves as she came in.

I'm driving and Zeus
quiet Zeus
in the passenger seat
head in a drunken bow:

"She was all right, wasn't she?"
     "Who? My cousin?"
"No, the girl I turned into a cow."

January Thaw

The tulips are too excitable, it is winter here.

1.

Tulip in a glass
The napkin by your place
Your voice spreads out
Surrounding vase
And tulip. Night
Calls beyond
The pane.

2.

Threads you keep finding and fingering,
following back to their origins
(where do the threads begin?)

Taut strings encircling rundles,
the frangible stones of your sculptures,
irregular pendulums gathering seconds of light.

Threads of this day without turning:
warp/woof/weft.
The spider's frozen web.

3.

From the southeast, the bluebirds come. By the dozens, they come.
Swooping, swirling, stopping, bluing. This 11th day of January
stopping here, rising and falling. Circling lilac, alighting magnolia
on fire. Bouncing and buoyant, believing in blueness and bugs.
Little boys blue, boys blue.

4.

In the glass
A woman reads a tulip
Beyond the spreading vase
The night tied in a napkin
Inside the pane
Little blue sadness,
Be still.

Zubarán Lemons, Oranges

That Sunday
Eduardo wanted to take me to a museum,
pictures inspire, he said, though of course
less than your skirt with its appliquéd shells,
your black hair, the silver glints,
your green eyes, your breasts,
the pictures, he repeated,
but said he was *resfriado* with the flu,
so please, please come over.
I took the metro, I took a bus,
I had oranges in my bag,
oranges the size of breasts, lemons,
Zubarán oranges, lemons.
I worried, will the neighbors
spy for my husband,
feed me quietly,
thrill to a quick end
to that quicksand desert,
but I was dressing to please,
tight skirt, short, my own clothes.
I was wearing bright pink,
carrying Zubarán oranges, lemons.

When I got there Eduardo was weak,
draped himself around me,
we were together on his purple
sofa, he traced my face, touched
everywhere, I will sicken, I said,
yes, he said, sicken with me.
I'll take you to bed,
and it was true,
I couldn't stop myself.
My body followed a logic,
but what? My husband might
hurt me like before
but here in this wishful space,
Eduardo began to eat lemons quietly,
bite ravenous oranges,
sicken me, sicken me,
lift me, feed me
and Eduardo, oh Eduardo,
somehow make me well.

The Bowl

The wall of the black bowl gathers behind you,
cool stone pressing your back, your arms
stretched, wrists turned, fingertips and palms
resisting the slow slipping down until – one time –
you say Okay, here is where I am, and let go.

The texture of the bowl a faint roughness
against your heels, buttocks and shoulder blades,
the air a stroking up the front of your body.

The curve increases, you wait for the bottom
that opens beneath you, dropping you
into the sky, into a blinding bearing-up light.

As though the sun rises only
above you, as though the dawn happens
outside your body.

Knowing, One More Time

A sudden wind
claims
the glass bowl
from the balcony's
ledge,
salad flying
down
fifty-six floors,
a watercolor
of spring greens,
pears,
pecans,
deep reds of tomatoes,
snow-like Asiago,
the bowl
turning
for an instant
as if to catch
what it had held,
and for that moment
I believe
in the bowl,
not accepting
that it will shatter
never to be
more
than jagged pieces,
the salad
falling
more slowly
to settle
with
the broken
glass.

Gypsy Davy's Flute of Rain

Gypsy Davy came along
He sang so strange and sweetly

I'd filled the final page of my diary
A lovely thing given to me by The Lady of the Lake
& bound in a cover of tooled leather

The color of late-summer heather
& a single emerald spiking up at its center

To signal the green eye of the peacock carved there
So jealously guarding my words

Jealousy jealousy oh yes so much of what
I'd written in its pages only fable after fable
Of men always at odds with the truth

Men whose belief in love was so unequivocally
Selfish & provisional
The slightest little breeze off the hem of a skirt
Flowed along the river of their dreams & slowly

I learned my job was to play just a little tune

On a flute of jade & rain
To sing a simple song about the end of pain

& if you read on you'll no doubt discover those ways

Such strange tender renders new life to any
Woman or man who'd follow a song beyond the beds
Of the forgotten
                        into lavish fields of blue light

Only the luckiest lovers may claim

Half-Dream, Sign & Rainwater

*

And I was half-full & half-empty,
as when the moon can be half-light, half-dream.

Like the phrase by Diane Arbus, "What's left
after what isn't is taken away."

When I reached into the dark & the scorpion stung me,
I could feel my heartbeat in my fingertip.

The wind through the trees sounds like the word *September*,
or a love letter kept in a drawer for twenty years.

The center of night is like Michelangelo's marble block;
the dream is found within its dark.

*

The puzzling sign above the slot machines in Reno
that reads, *You Must Be Present To Win.*

When Keats was my age he'd been dead
twenty-six years. He had his mid-life crisis at twelve.

Why does the nothing that follows the something
disturb me more than the nothing before the nothing?

And then one night you find yourself in a motel in Las Cruces
with a missing letter M. The neon flashing OTEL, OTEL, OTEL.

"Oh, you'll live," they say.
No, I won't.

*

The ticking watch on the stiffened wrist of the dead man
is not a contradiction.

Rainwater tracing the etched names
& dates on burial monuments.

And life, Nelly Sachs wrote to Paul Celan,
has always tasted like farewell.

Bitterness is when you throw a stone today
trying to kill yesterday's bird.

Salt is pain. Water is regret.
If I had to do it over, I'd do it over.

Trinity A Woman

Old jim third
or fourth generation
still out there on
old trinity
road to the plantation

Old jim listed
in the 1984 white pages
dare i phone you
from the holiday inn

Come as far back as
a yellow fever epidemic
done as much as i can
in this dead rivertown's
courthouse and library

Dare i ride out that
red road to trinity now
a mulatto woman
alone in a hertz

Talking slavery
and rape
asking about henrietta
and polly

(polly "died" in childbirth
perhaps never marrying the mysterious
mr. pharoah savage
aunt retta like a mother
to mama "disappeared" in 1916)

Old jim third what
would you do
come a black woman
orphaned to trinity
what say
i begged a peek a
our family bible?

Sign People

All torso and angled appendage,
their disc heads floating
on thin rims of collar.

Black-and-yellow tenants of the school zone,
faceless loiterers at crosswalks, at least
their lavatory cousins are gendered:
the males' four blunt limbs,
the females in bell-skirts
with their perfect posture.

How unlike us, these shadows
of caution and propriety, presuming to lead
without feet, hands, eyes.

Road Service

Rita's mouth dropped
at the unexpected full-load
pickup pulling off, squealing,
onto the shoulder beside her little
coupe. *Lucky I came by*, Harry, the
name on his shirt, said, sauntering
out of the well-equipped truck. How
could he not, given his profession, notice
her classic chassis in need? Rita tried to take it
all in, mooning over the sight of his bulging
black extended cab 4x4. *Give me a jump?*
She felt around for the latched slot to
pop her hood, which Harry instantly
knew where to find, his thick fingers slip-
ping under her grill. *Oh*, she blurted. One
hand above her head, the other raising the rod
that would prop open her hood, Rita stretched,
leaning over her exposed motor, Harry's breath
on her neck. Jumper cables he kept in his bed snaked
around his arms, he licked his lips. *We'll*, he winked,
get you going. She smiled, sure he knew what went
where & how. His engine throbbing, the jagged teeth
of the cables gently bit the hard nodes of her battery. *Now*,
he yelped. Door swung wide, left foot on the ground, her
right on the gas, key in the ignition, she pumped a bit
wildly, turning over & over until a series of faltering flutters
reached a high-pitched crescendo & shook her car. *How much
do I owe you?* Rita asked, relieved. *Not a damn thing*, Harry shot back.
He gunned his engine. Rita, aglow, gushed even as he sped off, long
after the waggle of his tailgate shrank to just a smudge in her rear view.

My brother chose to carve
his marriage into this,
the lake's beech – a small
violence in the bark. Over
the years the silt has grown
the lake bed and his carving
pushed out
by new growth inside
making his love
illegible, a secret language,
a place he can return
and point to and say here
is the scar where my love
used to be.

Mackerel Sky

Under the morning's usual noise, the quarrels
of creek and trucks, a saw
insists its way through bark, taking down
the poplar. Circles inside the circle
of its trunk, like ripples a coin makes,
face up, face down,
falling. Seems we can only look
a little at a time, tenderness
has to surprise me, as the sheep did,
driven sudden from their barn, seamless confusion
of eyes & hooves & wool.
They looked frightened, but maybe
that was me, not knowing,
and the scaly clouds so close –
         which is to say I want to learn
to love you better, in this drift
of sawdust so fine and light
that, though the season's wrong,
for a moment I think it's snow.

Sixty O'Clock

1.

Is it a ripsaw in hardwood spitting
a burst of sawdust, a spray
of pent-up

woodchips? That nagging
two-note, is it a hopeless car engine
that won't turn over,

or a bird? Could it be a bird?
Or is it a siren grinding
its monomaniacal

hardluck story at the corner
or closer, at the steamed-up
window I wake to?

2.

The house is chilly when I get home.
I rattle inside it like ice cubes in the tray.
November. Any day now
will blow the trees bare.

In morning, light stokes up
the red-leaf Japanese maple.

If it weren't so cold out
I could warm myself
at a fire like that.
If the left hand would not push away
what the right desires. If the cold
were a little less cold –

A distance stops short and
listens, a wild distance that has caught
my scent.

Merrill

After his death
the Ouija board still spoke sometimes
to his friends. Gibberish,
they decided, something only he
could decipher. One day it spoke
in sentences instead of lists of words –
Cricket earphones fail us not
it spelled out. *The girders*
of the mind, it said, were *twisted,*
as if he were speaking
from the other side.
And why not? He had believed
it could be done – messages in a language
only poets and psychics understood.
And weren't they the same sort,
whose flesh seemed made
of language, whose words
burned? But there was no time
to analyze causes or connections.
The board was on the move.
Do not sweep me
downstream with the stars,
it spelled out. *You are the heroes*
without name or origin.
Was it he, they wondered
as their hands were pulled
over the letters fast, faster,
or his muse? Or was it only
themselves missing him
the way he would bring back
moments of his own life –
palpable – though made only
of words, of poems?

NOTE: Italicized lines are from James Merrill's "Under Mars," "Grace," "Banks of
a Stream Where Creatures Bathe," and "Scenes of Childhood," respectively.

falling rain

for Philip Lamantia

a blind man walking in a city is a black bird flying through a burning forest. a black bird flying through a burning forest is a street map to a blind man. a blind man is a black bird flying at night through a burning forest who recognizes the smell of rain.

in fact it is night. in fact it is raining. in fact a black bird flying through a burning city is a streetmap of rain to a blind man. in fact a blind man at night in rain recognizes the streets of a city like the back of his hand.

in fact a blind man who recognizes the tender smell of rain in a burning forest is a black bird. in fact the back of a blind man's hand is a burning forest when a black bird is flying through it.

a black bird is instinctual. a blind man stepping off a curb into the streets of a city is instinctual. rain falling in a burning forest at night is instinctual.

a blind man walking through a city is rain falling in a burning forest.

a tattoo of a black bird on the back of a blind man's hand is falling rain.

Bending Twice

Twice he stooped and wrote in
dust. The first time was to cause
a brief diversion, give him time
to think, and so he bent and maybe listed
all the places he would rather be,
then stood and told the sinless to
take up their stones.

The second time would be
the mystery – the hot-eyed crowd
gone sheepish, breaking up –
if it weren't that I've done the same
when something flickered in
a word: thrown down a tool,
pulled off the road, gone back
and bent again, the sky no bluer
for whatever came.

With Style

Dylan Thomas and I got drunk on the same night
in the same city, only he did it with style.
He stood at the bar downing shot after shot
while reciting the poems of Thomas Hardy
in that voice that filled the world. Meanwhile
in a hotel room off Washington Square I sat
staring out the window as the night came on
wondering what I was doing. Late September,
his time was running out, and mine wasn't,
yet he was full of fire and language and I –
not yet twenty-six – couldn't even cry out
against the evening falling between the trees.
When the filthy window gave back only me,
the bedside table with its lamp, the silent TV,
and no more, I thought I was seeing into myself.
I wasn't. When I closed my eyes I saw half
of what was there. When he closed his did he see
my darkness? His own darkness? Or did he see
from the hills above Swansea the world he'd left,
the small houses crowded together like children
afraid of their parents, the church steeple, tiny
from so far off, the harbor, the deepening sea
as dusk settled in and separate lights came on?

Hidden Man

Biddy thought he might be a Hidden Man when
he was taking a leak in the snow and realized he
was writing some of T. S. Eliot's stuff, for real,
Kaminsky asked and Biddy said, yeah, some
unseen force just grabbed his banana and started
scribbling like mad, in fact he covered miles through
the low country and even relieved himself of Eliot's
silhouette before he was through and knew what
the goddamn thing was all about, he was a *Lamed
Vodnik*, a hero standing between the Jews, Eliot
and the end of time.

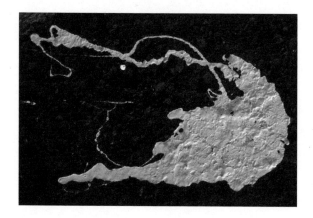

The Measure of Sorrow

For Larry Levis

Fireflies caught in a jar die.
A child mourns the passing light.
Your father dies, your name on his lips
each syllable a curse. Or so you imagine.
A clumsy Salsa, all left feet with your lover
never finding the right cadence.
A filterless cigarette burning and the café
facing the river on a cold Parisian
evening cannot bear the weight.
What words can be said to rain and night
and a car speeding through both?
Three lines stolen from you, old gypsy
Magician at his own revival
Here are all the shadows that have fallen,
A single window smashed and bare with sky.

Mission Statement of the Empty Notebook

Between the Lines of the Empty Notebook

The empty notebook reads between its lines
and learns that time is space, that rumors are
secrets wrapped in lies, that truth comes in
and out of focus, wisdom is born from every
perspective, information rides in all directions,
but reaches its destination lost, white is not
an absence of hue, but every color blended,
and black every color pushing to take its turn,
while every lie is waiting for its truth to get off
the bus. The empty notebook declares amnesty.

Suspicions of the Empty Notebook

The empty notebook never sleeps;
it's counting sheep, getting in shape for
life on the shelf as a vigilant witness.
The empty notebook feels under attack
when the moon's weft floats over the floor,
it tries to alert its neighbors – jiggling
pencils, riffling pages, spitting staples.
When the moon's slant slices the room,
the empty notebook calls the police, who
treat the case as domestic dispute, but
the empty notebook has its suspicions.
It wants the moon under arrest.

The Empty Notebook in Paris

The empty notebook bustles down
boulevards, roams through twenty
rooms of the Louvre and scuttles
into the Metro, where it rides to all
destinations. At the Café de Flore, a
young woman nods and orders wine.
Hubba hubba, whispers the notebook,
and hopefully, Scribble scrabble?
The woman picks up a pencil, draws
a key, a church, a heart on the front
of the notebook, then an apple, a tree,
a bridge, a knife. The empty notebook
thinks, what did she mean by that?
All of the sudden its cover is lifted
by the painted nail of the woman's
little finger. She leaves an imprint
of her hand on the notebook's
blank page and the heat of her hand
turns the smooth page to gooseflesh,
the force of her hand tosses the notebook
into a satchel, hustles it down the length
of the Rue St.-Benoît to a tree by a bridge
on the river, where it is fingered, caressed,
cut and kissed until it forgets it is empty.

The Empty Notebook in Prison

Dogs are barking.
The empty notebook flinches,
stripped of its cover, stacked
on a pile, wired and heated,
hoodwinked and prodded,
it hears screams with flickers
of laughter. A smirk rounds
the corner and raps on the bars
with an automatic weapon.
Fizzle and crack of electroshock
static rakes the frail air
while sweet rot staunches
the empty notebook's resolve
to quench empty questions
with meaningless answers.
Time to take notes. Time to spill
guts. Time for the tearing of fresh
spiral bindings. The empty notebook
quivers in its pile of notebooks,
trying to stay hidden, trying to stay
blank. Bared teeth. The empty
notebook lets go of its margins,
insists on beginning again.

The Empty Notebook and Immortality

The empty notebook knows its
only talent is emptiness, but wishes for
pages blue with writing while imagining
an afterlife: on file, recycled, scrapped,
in storage. It dreams reincarnation,
encyclopedia, checkbook, newspaper,
document, cinder flying out of the ashes.
The empty notebook looks for a signal
for everything to unravel – a point,
a line, a start to any story, an indication
of a phrase, a word, a letter – anywhere
speech leaves its droppings. It knows
how sound disappears between pages,
but the shape it has taken remains.

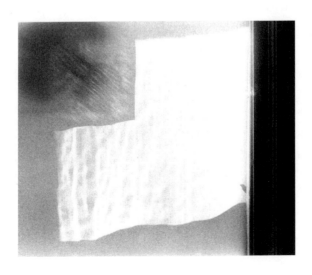

Mi Vida

My life is a tangled skein of moments
for which I have mostly avoided being present,
looking forward and backward, running messages
from past to future. Memories are silver
fish darting in the shallows, whales
that surface from holding their breath
in the deep green waters of childhood.

My mother's a ghost with my daughter's face,
an unextinguished fire in the hollow of time.
My father's a deep-sea salesman peddling
sperm to the whales, snow to the Eskimos,
violins to the deaf, and a deck of cards
to gamblers who have just lost their last penny.

Others are coming and going in these rooms
and after sixty years I am just beginning
to be able to distinguish their voices.
Jealousy is neither here nor there.
Fear is a robot with two faces, adding up
to zero. History is a newspaper
we can use to compost the tomatoes.

Love is a book with no pages, a song
with no rhymes, sugar in my coffee,
an endless journey approaching
the present moment as a limit. Poetry
is the vowel of wave-crash, the consonant of the sun,
the torch I pass on to the children, spilling sparks.

תַּרְנְגֹלֶת לְבָנָה

White chicken

בְּאֶמְצַע יוֹם הֵי
אֲנִי עוֹמֶדֶת כְּתַרְנְגֹלֶת
עַל מַזְלְגוֹת רַגְלַי

In the middle of
Thursday
I stand like a chicken
on the forks of my legs

לוּ הָיְתָה פֹּה
לְפָחוֹת
מְרִיצַת גַּלְגַּלִּים
אֲדֻמָּה
מְזֻגֶּגֶת בְּמֵי
גֶּשֶׁם
הָיִיתִי מַלְבִּינָה
לְצִדָּהּ
בְּאֹפֶן גּוֹרָלִי

if at least
I had
a red
wheelbarrow
glazed with rain
water
I would whiten
beside it
fatefully

אֲבָל כָּךְ
בְּמַצָּבִי
אֵינִי מַעֲלָה
וְאֵינִי מוֹרִידָה
דְּבָרִים
אֶלָּא חַיָּה
לְרָעָתִי
עִם הַכַּרְבֹּלֶת
עַל רֹאשִׁי.

but this way
in my situation
I effect
no change
rather I live,
not for my own sake,
with a cockscomb
on my head.

Secret Languages

There are languages we think we know:
the whale's serenade of its mate;
the crude letters bears scratch on bark as warning;
the panther's piss marking its address in sand;
the sonar chorus of bats echoing in the night;
the never-quite-ready symphony of crickets fine-tuning instruments.

And languages we hardly know:
the frenzied dance of bees;
the rainbow blush of cuttlefish;
the scent-configured chemistry of pheromones;
the serpent's lexicon of tongue;
the skeletal illuminations of deep ocean fish.

And some may be more language than we think:
the starlings group-flight, an office meeting on the wing;
the schooling of herring, a semaphore run of scales;
the unto-death silence of the swan broken by the elegant mime of its neck;
the psychedelic throbbing of jellyfish from the world's unconscious;
the writhing of snakes, a picture language of desire.

Are there others we never guessed?
Does the tiger flex its stripes in code?
The elephant sprays moist suggestions on the backs of the herd?
Is the warm texture of hair, a subtle language of touch?
Does the oyster speak in slow dark rhythms of mud?

And might not there be a language of stone
played to the ocean's crescendo along the shore?
And doesn't rain make wet music with the earth?
And aren't the Moon's phases
a four-bar ballad sung to earth from the Sun?

Montecore Speaks

I was never your friend
nor were you mine
what you saw in my eyes
not love but patience

> *in the taiga silent passage*
> *between old trees*
> *striation of light, shadow*
> *crust of crystals on deep snow*

panthera tigris alpaica suspended
spinning globe in rising stage fog
did you imagine this was a life
this obscenity this amusement
for lovers of slots and lapdance
while you collected applause
I collected myself

> *tracks in the river mud*
> *a flattened blade of grass*
> *slow rain penetrating*
> *the dense understory*
> *genetic memory of sky*

now you know
what was illusion.

Montecore: seven year old Siberian tiger in the illusionist act of
"Siegfried & Roy"

All My Relations

Cousin Hawk:

First the shadows of
your
        talons
meet the mouse.

Cousin Porcupine:

Little
        walking
nettle-bush.

Cousin Io-Moth:

Here's
        looking at
you
too.

Cousin Skunk:

Please
        don't
turn your
back on me.

Cousin Snake:

Nobody knew
you had your
new suit
        on
too
until you left
your old
        empty one
here.

The Turtles of La Escobilla

With machetes, the men hack
at the green sea turtles.
They shoot them with long rifles.
They take them away on their horses
whole and squirming in the moonlight.
They dig their eggs out of the sand.
They laugh and drink tequila.

Still, the turtles come back,
ciphers of the earth,
tsunamis of creation,
for 200 million years
a pattern in the void,
raw wet shoulders rising
from the broken shells.

Rising as each man stumbles
in the house to hang up his belt,
rising like the fires of flesh,
crates of carapace,
rising bright and willing because,
like the moon, for most of time
the earth has been theirs.

Parting

The bear returned to her dreams after years of absence.
It begins the same: the tug of his desire and her longing for danger

hold them fast. As always, she escapes in a twist
of wrists and hips. This time a spear of rib bone grows from her hand

and she kills the bear, fearing for her mind. He smells of grass
and crushed olives. Daily bathing in underground pools of minerals and coal

has made him sleek as an otter. She reaches to touch him,
only to be hurled into space, wheeling through a future

bound by dunes and sea water. Here she revives the bear
with pomegranate seeds and hovering moths. He wails at the water's edge

and slips in. She wakes in an astonished looseness, walks
as a foreigner through her day. From the hills she views the bay through breaks

in the branches of pines and redwoods. Below, cranes lifting
containers off tankers are tender and beautiful, the pulleys oiled and silent.

Hunting on a Literary License

The bull moose raises a broad, dripping nose
from the feeding pond, his dark eyes keep watch
like sad sentinels, flash with the menace
of one who need step aside for nothing
and no one. The poet knows safety requires
distance, knows that the bull signals charge
with a drop of the head, that he hates dogs
because they come as wolves do, low-slung,
packed with purpose. The poet is upright, alone,
edges through the damp grasses and sedges
toward the shallows where the bull grazes,
rippling his rut-carved shoulder muscles.
The poet uncaps pen, opens notebook,
crouches low, like wolf, like dog, stalks closer,
and closer yet. There is no stopping now,
no going back. The bull drops his head.

Crossing

Driving through the greener suburbs, my brain
full of stops, I came upon a yellow sign
announcing, pictorially, that just ahead
was a duck crossing.
                              You can't imagine
my sudden happiness, to be reminded
simply of ducks, that ducks are with us,

and what's more, that they might, this very moment,
duckwalk single file across my path, that I
would need to yield, use unusual care.
What else makes a person
turn off the radio and quack the rest of the way home?

Raymond Carver

1938-1988
Salisbury, Maryland

5 a.m.: he slippers downstairs for coffee, one joint,
some rest after not sleeping
again, not drinking, after phone calls & late night talk:
the colleague whose petition
for promotion cited his reading *The New York Times*
"on a daily basis," then
listed prestigious journals that had rejected work.
Jeez, Ray had grinned, head shaking.
The dog scratches itself up off the wooden floor, cocks
its head at this soft touch, this
gentle goofball, whines *out?* – so Ray props open the door
for this mutt who has never
been outside without its chain, who pads onto the porch
fronting our busy street, turns
back just as Ray lets the screen door shut, then slowly slinks
off to some great adventure.

Hours later, I'm jogging the block, jingling an empty
leash, shouting "Bobby?" while Ray
crisscrosses the neighborhood in his cramped Volkswagen.
Did we find the dog? Of course –
it leapt onto his front seat, then panted home to sprawl
belly-up by the fireplace,
legs flung open in some canine parody of bliss.
In 1979
Bobby was still alive, Ray was still alive, my wife
slept through that particular
commotion, we all ate breakfast in the sunny nook
while the days ahead gathered
into "gravy," Ray called them, into poems & stories…
& Ray sits at the table,
laughing again, shaking his head, *Can you believe it?*
Jeez, what was that guy thinking?

Testimony of Dog

Windows open, doors ajar, my love,
A tinge of roast bird greasing the air –
Yet I don't ask for morsels of white meat,
More dried pig's ear or bone.
Instead, the bird, feathers and all, the whole beast.
To touch the dead is what I need,
To taste.
I want to dig and bury it deep,
Know crumble of earth and scumble of worm.
No restraints or complaints,
Here in the wood and deep in the duff,
O partner in grime, feral double of mine.

Flicking the red-rag of tongue,
Dreaming the hopeful dreams of dog,

Here we two loll, not rough, but among
The roots and above our death.
Here the air's clear – both cool and hot –
Snake-shade sharp-fringed with sun.
Beneath us, the dead unleash their whims
And fill us with breath. So fiercely,
We bay, shake body and spirit,
Deliver the gospel of dog.
Here lies.... Here we lie.
Here we don't ever have to lie again.

Past a thousand chewed-up scraps of time,
Song of the scent of the dead alive.

Here we worship, Old Dog, old anagram.
Yes, here over the dead and deep
In duff. Here we speak in tongues,
Yelp, moan, cry, howl.
Here, just here, us – above the dead.
We dance, we chant, we chance.
Yes, here –
In the deep and dark of the duff.

Fractal

A hand defines an oval,
A foot, a plane,
An ankle, an angle.

The spider, thus, the crenellated surface,
The snake, the coiling nautilus,
A grackle, a crackle.

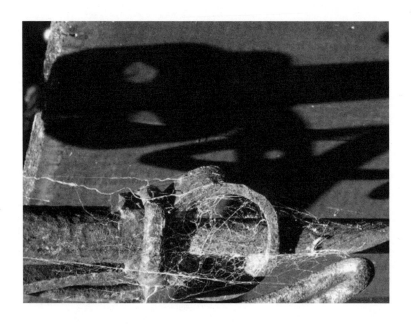

Spiritus

Possum, postulant, tell me you're simply playing
dead. You rise to swagger past trashcans, cars, picking your
way on scaly feet (four-fingered, dark, sharp) back out
into the fray. *Come what may.* Waft of the barn cats' kibble
drew you to the stoop where under a bare bulb
flicked on and off, you rattled the plastic dish that called us out
to witness your bumbling (rosary of your tracing), your clumsy
unintended descent: grey football, end to end over the top
step. Your tail a mangy tap-root, a scraped parsnip pocked
with garden dirt, your pointed, pink, wedge-shaped head,
your pale snout gleaming through pewter wire tufts
and pressed to concrete. Blind to our flurry. We have nothing
but the empty dish of our hearts. You don't scare at the door's
click; you circle, sniff, befuddled and unperturbed.

    That something can lie so still yet live. There's hope.

Double Wedding Ring

How cramped a lot
to be a slave-stitched quilt,
to be Cathedral Church in cast-off gingham, or
old Shoofly sewn in blocks of red
and studded with a dirty pinwheel heart.
How wretched to
be born from tattered scraps
of common cotton cloth and penny thread to form
dark sheets of patchwork squares. How small
and mocking to be *comforter,* though frail
and thin. By night,
to rest on worn-out laps
and later beds and bodies in attempts to cut
cold cabin winds... and then, by day,
to hang against wind-splintered fence rails, or
along the backs
of peeling porch chairs, there
to air under the harsh spilled Southern sun. Bow Ties,
Log Cabin, Flying Geese: stitched fast
from cloth, one at a time, the quilts displayed

their solemn, spot-
stained fronts. How sore a fate! The dazed parade
of masters, mules, and slaves looked past
the fence-draped quilts; just one or two cast up their eyes
in quickened glance to where
the quilts hung lax.
Those certain sharp-eyed few knew to look for
the Monkey Wrench *(go hide away*
the tools), to recognize good Wagon Wheel *(pack what*
is needed), next perhaps
to note the bright
zigzags of Drunkard's Path *(stagger your trail)*,
and then, one day, to see the fall
and rise of Tumbling Boxes *(leave tonight)*. Not warm
those quilts (all shred and gaps),
not expert (too
coarse, primitively sewn), not song, not art…
but, hanging there, those blankets read
as eloquent as prose: their patchwork words free-born
from thread, their phrases built
from stitch and knot.

Sota de copas
(recordatorio)

Despues de cruzar la palma con plata,
    despues del truhán,
        la sota de copas:
   es estudioso
       el paje que ofrece la copa,
          que trae el recado.
    Piensa en él, medítalo bien:
no se sabe si se rebosará la copa
o si en el fondo sólo heces
de un vino ya agotado.
    Tómala
       que para bendecir
         hasta con agua.

Knave of Cups
(reminder)

After crossing the palm with silver,
    after the Fool,
       the Knave of Cups:
   the page who offers the cup,
       who brings the message,
         is studious.
    Think on him, reflect:
it is not known
if the cup will run over
or if there be in the bottom
only the lees of an exhausted wine.
    Take it
       that for a blessing
         even water will do.

Magi

Houses are impossible anymore.
There is a shout in the Christmas trees,
And he is a strong man.

In the cold street,
A discarded chair faces the Sachem Apartments,
And it begins to be a book –

Orphaned by Indians,
Boyhood buddies meet again
When they are strong men,
& the writing desks shatter at their touch,
& rocking horses float on frozen air, hunting,
& Christ is a stronger man shouting in the trees.

The year 2005.
All the orphans have refused our houses.
I see them in the street
In the broken chairs at broken desks.
The splintered wood speaks to them.
It soothes them, I can see that.
And as it happens,
I do not wish to see anything else anymore.

Distress Signals in a Time of War

And though, since that time, I have read many books,
have followed the smoke trail of countless thoughts
rising from the burning libraries,
though I have inquired in the ruins of many cities,
in the writing on the fallen walls,
in the blank stares of skulls in the killing fields,
in places hidden and open:
Nevertheless, I do not understand.

For though, when as a child, I watched the news unreel
at the movies: the smoke and guns, the stirring symphonic music
rousing the blood, the black and white legions marching
on film, the flare of anti-aircraft guns, the little planes turning
in a slow spiral as they went down in flames, the heavy-bellied
bombers opening their doors, and the bombs falling,
and where each one fell, a rising pillar of fire; and though
the voice of the announcer was manly and confident, the news
always good, we were winning, we were certainly winning, and
everyone was so proud, and collected cans, and went without
nylons and chewing gum and butter, and clustered around radios
speaking in hushed tones as if in a holy place:
Nevertheless I did not understand.

And though, since that time, I have followed Freud's trail, and Adler's,
tracked bad parents, bacteria, the rotting culture in the petri dish,
followed Nietzche to the knife in Raskolnikov's hand, with Pip
have seen God's foot on the treadle of the loom, watched goats lick
the pillar of salt that is the whole history of grief; though
I have followed Socrates into the bathhouses of Athens, observed
how he drank the poison that certainty decrees to skepticism;
though I have watched 10,000 Iagos ply their cunning trade
of betrayal; though I have looked in my own heart,
and knowing myself no better than most, and worse than many,
nevertheless, I do not understand.

For, today, when I follow the signs of distress
back to their source, I find only mourners
weeping at the cemetery we have made
of what was once their home.
And playing in the rubble, a little girl
who will never understand, who
nevertheless
is picking up stone after stone,
trying to piece it together again.

At the Child Abuse Symposium

1st Slide
The pathologist had removed her ribs
and ranged them on a tray. Red arrows
point to the bone-bumps of healed
and healing fractures. Even I, an outsider,
can see the fresh breaks.

2nd Slide
She lies on a table, her head turned
to the side, distancing herself
from the autopsy. I see how
her soul had flown to her bedroom
window and clung to the sill
until he stopped. After that she kept
the window open a crack –
one night her soul flew away.

3rd Slide
She sits at her desk, her classmates a blur
of motion behind her. A cupcake
and a small wrapped gift sit before her
untouched. She will not smile
for the camera. Was even the one
who took this photo looking the other way?

Emblems of Memory

Gaza

girls suspend portraits
pendants
    around their necks

    like Victorian ladies holding the lost
    in broaches at their throats
        each breath saying his name

even the young ones recite martyrs
better than multiplication, heroes to emulate
    exploding corsets of death

        the locket bears a hidden picture, a snippet
        of hair, each woman's private
        act of affection

unlike the soul at the throat of
an ordinary girl, too fresh for love but
    not for desiring her face

        emblazoned across amulets
        a very public display of
        defiance

From The Dark Country

Yes, there were signs. Men began to gather,
women sighed. Children asked questions we
couldn't answer. That winter our town swelled
like a bruise – soldiers filled the churches
and schools. Stories came from Zeitoun
and Erzurum. Police watched the streets.
One day our teacher was taken and returned
dumb. My mother wrapped him in fresh goat skin
to heal the wounds. So stories fled our town,
became warnings for people we didn't know.

Yet there were signs more fearful and sure,
sent by neither Turk nor Armenian.
As I hung laundry in the morning sun,
a back bird perched on the wire and I knew.

~

Cruelty can be given a shape
in the sweltering minds of men.
Given language it shows up on paper
and in mouths. It can travel on roads
and wires, arrive cloaked in streets
of distant cities: dispassionate, a job,
orders carried out in service of a name.

Yet some acts have no flag, no religion.
No code binds them. With nothing
to gain, no goal to achieve, they result
from no particular demands. Some acts
are simply dark, human things
for which no explanation stands –
a corpse without hands, a bag of tongues.

~

If I recite for you the prayers and pleas,
recall, as I am cursed with the capacity
to do, the forms a starving body takes
on its way to death, what would it solve?
Such memories have their own language,
known only by those who lived
their creation. Oh you can go back,
mark some places they fell, find a bed
of poppies where an orchard once stood.
But where would be the melting corpses,
the cries of infants snuffed out by fire,
or those still walking toward the end, their eyes
sunk deep, steeped in what they have seen?

~

To be told, it had to survive, as one man
dry as dust clings to something human
inside him. In the desert, history
evaporates as soon as it happens
and what can be read in the bones
left behind always points someplace else.
Go there and you will not find me.
I was not the land I walked on nor
the house I lived in. The words I used
were not mine, just as the people I loved,
who fled in all four directions of the wind,
did not know me. An Armenian voice
can blend with the sound of a slow wind.
Some stories are not told in words.

Currency

In that time

    in isolate rooms

of brow-beaten cities   dirt-sodden villages   grimy towns

each put a hand in a pocket   opened a drawer

        rummaged in a purse

    took out the coin

        and set it on end

some on the floor   on mirror   on a table

    some on the back of the hand

        tip of the nose

            nail of the large toe

        flat of an arm

in some places some went outdoors to spin their coins

at the curb of the lane   on the sidewalk

                on the slate of a garden path

on rooftops
                at the foot of mountains

                        into caves and low valleys

earth barnacled with coin

                priceless denominators

                        gathering momentum

                ceaseless   tireless

ONECOINANOTHERCOINANOTHERCOINANOTHER

The Flagrant Dead

on the earliest photographic erotica

And here, too, are the libertines, the demi-reps,
of Finsbury Park and the Haymarket streets,
the gardens of pleasure in Cremorne and Soho,
with their gas-lit circles, crystal, and kiosks.
Reduced, long-dead, they incline, they awaken;
look, their earliest eyes, wide open, or seeming so,
from the bog-house, the cesspool, of sin,
stare back at us, demanding that we watch.

And in their eyes is the absolute suspension
of the pose, skirts lifted, knee socks down,
thick erection poised, its bold inaction held,
while an open shutter gathers in the light.
The women are supine or offer to be mounted,
staring back or up, and some with smiles,
while the men, their unbuttoned trousers
trenched below their thighs, shirt tails trailing,
heavy suspenders undone, lean forward,
toward and around the dark inviting center.
What strikes us most are the faces turned,
the looks of invitation in the dead immediate,
the easy letting-go of all reserve.

Against this put pretense: nymphs and satyrs,
lovers on a swing or fleeing the sudden storm,
the moment when a dear intended paused,
her duty in the balance, to contemplate her heart.
Think, too, of how Rossetti made his wife
the "Blessed Beatrice" of his charged desire;
recall, as well, young Alice's unbudded charm,
arranged just so, all pose, all likelihood.
Instead these images perform themselves;
these dead, like lunatics, avert no appetite;
their under-petticoats, their corded dimity
adorned like turkey-work, their pin-up coats
of Scotch plaid, tricked with bugle lace,
their gowns of printed calico, come off,
dead-level, down to this; no lace-trimmed
cambric shirt, no silk cravat, no beauty wash,
no essences of jasmine, keep all fresh,
in struggles long and hard against undress.

What anxious thought inhibits us tonight?
What dread of illness or of slouching gait?
Whose eyes are these, and whose attractive lips?
In mirrors, as we watch, our masks dissolve,
our glasses fill with spirited champagne;
we please ourselves to praise the flagrant dead,
to celebrate the vintage of their spending.

Spectator at Gandhi's Assassination

Ahimsa! A sound sibilant and atmospheric
meant for no jalsa, or God-fearing men
in the mood for prolonged discourse.

Violence shades into nonviolence
by gradations too pure to be defined.

Next day, a riot will burst loose.

How bad is a day's pea soup
for a man fed only on promises?

Then, memories of the salt drive,
homespun, sickness in prison
brought on by the little man
who refused to fill his shoes.

The final gunshot perfection,
home like the dead's prayer.

Pillow

Every night,
our heads reach for infinity.

The subconscious
flies without fettles
across the galaxy, past this world of consciousness,
this world of morals and customs.

The pillow fires that freedom
and carries our unconscious like a satellite,
gathering memories
as it goes.

It's just like our feet wearing shoes:
the head rides the pillow,
flying
over limitless space
so different from the distances traveled by feet,

clutching soft, feathery dreams.

– translated from the Korean by Steven J. Stewart, Scott Slovic, and the author

To Fence With Time

when the dialogues began
we were the children of the future

singing songs of thanksgiving
although the words were strange in our mouths

until memory bathed us
and light stretched one wing

and some alien blessing was on its way
a voice born in captivity

older than water a light rising from loss
extinguishing the dark

we built a roof with our hands
wove walls to stop the wind

painted windows
each with its kingdom

and the doors
open to the sun

we wove a cage of wishes
arcing against time

the moon chalked its zeros
as we merged unencumbered

until the sun dusted the earth with gold
where every leaf was mute

the shell of oblivion tight
and the circle made perfect

Heft

I hold the words *broken bones*
in my hand; I hold the word
ribcage, the word *heart*.
I lift every word
like a stone or a feather.

The more beautiful words,
like *heaven*, or *nothingness*,
feel exactly the same
as *fencepost* or *mailbox*,
lamplight or *shoelace*.

Spirit
flits like a tongue of flame,
as insubstantial in the hand
as its brother, *death*,
which weighs exactly the same as *life*.

After Candle Time

Soon after candle time, when pines
push new tips sunward, late in June,
just as summer shifts from promise
to performance, on the second day
of ruby-throats and laurel bloom,
while camping on a wooded northern face
near the crest of Pinchot Ridge, I woke
to what has become last blood,
a stain like rust on a leafstalk.
Is this how worlds change,
one element transforming another?
How what is rooted, earth-bound
takes to air, borne by spore.

Between my legs a new scent –
chapatti, kavli, bread without yeast,
yet sporish, as if the vigorous mold
of physical decline
had cultivated new growth,
as if something young
had sprung from decay,
like the foxfire, bloodroot,
the shy monkshood
that thrive in the mulch of fallen laurel,
fragrant flourishes of shade.

Sundown

Like a dragonfly in slow motion
dipping one double wing after the other,
she kayaks the lake, braced and deliberate
as Danae through the golden gift. Birds hush.
The surrounding trees flaunt their last rags
of October while their sky-water selves
– deeper selves – tremble under her passing.
In and out of the sun's lessening light,
she paddles to the engine of her own breathing,
pivoting her upper body with each dip of the oar.
And the lake, stirred by the willow wand
of that straight back, that metronome, that baton
of loveliness, cannot help but puddle around her
and drink – pearl in a goblet – the final wink of the day
down.

What is she thinking alone on the lake,
what wrinkle in the brain, download of memory,
keeps her company, distracting her enough
so Beauty can take her unawares, clothe
her naked artlessness in such shining?
What's beauty worth on today's market
that each action is executed as if it were
primordial connection, the golden clasp – pay dirt
we could take to the bank, endorse, cash in?
And how do I fit in this picture? Heart-
hiding behind a tree, furiously scribbling
as if anyone but three people and a duck
cared what I – sustained by walking these last
remnants of wildness – record, report,
think.

No matter. I say this corner of the world
waits for her, depends on her for its daily
now I lay me down. That the loitering sun
kills time tucking the finches, under
where their pillows are. They say in China
in the emptying choirs of these trees, eating
the bitter berries of exile, singing all day
in long sad columns of Mandarin, impatient
until she comes – half woman, half boat – creature
of another element with her dragon stick
that propels through the trap door of this lake
the go-between that loves them – brass-tongued
emissary, the sky's gong – beaming their messages
home.

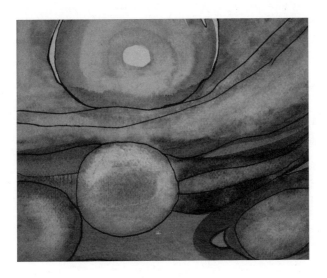

Supposing, for Instance, Here
in the Space-Time Continuum

Maybe – if we lie here a little longer, letting our toes
        Touch in the late fashion of preadolescent bluebirds
Or lovers, squaring their bodies to whatever melody
        The water makes, gurgling against rocks, a few twigs

And the broken beer bottle that, given its proximity
        To the bank, & the fair-to-moderate clip the current
Cuts around the bend, scoring the glass to an almost
        Delicate green, could *almost* be beautiful – supposing

For instance, time carries all things towards a point
        Of departure, & the old man feeding carrier pigeons
Will one day die, the last bits of a sandwich, glazing
        His upper lip & the lapels of his suit, tired & serving

No practical purpose after fifty-six years of working
        Numbers into columns, into vacations & sports cars
He'd never indulged in, selling even the old Chrysler
        He cut to the curb each morning, on the hill outside

The bakery, where he'd sometimes stop – for coffee,
        Or a muffin – & later, letting the tires roll a few feet
Before popping the clutch & heading towards home,
        After the death of the dancer, he'd refused to marry,

Though they'd shared a house together once, before
        The cancer crept back into her breast, & his pension
Proved too little to support them both – suggesting,
        Perhaps to some extent, mutual separation, distance,

The cold hard facts of life, the way an old man looks
        After his car has been bought & sold & towed away,
The lines on his face growing hard – then blemishing
        To a softness like leaves, like fire . . . that misfortune

A person must feel, watching his whole house go up
        In flames, & *realizing* – standing under the streetlight
Where the snow seems to fall the hardest & the cars,
        Slowing to watch as fire climbs the walls & windows,

The asphalt shingles of the roof, seem almost frozen
        For a moment, like statuaries, against so much snow
– *how* inconsequential it all must seem to the firemen,
        Working overtime & on call & this far into the night,

And how, when the first floor gives, the whole thing
        Will come crashing down . . . not in tears, or blurred
By fire – but in the sudden shudder of pigeon wings,
        Taking flight, lifting their big, dumb bodies in the air,

And then settling back down – strutting the tall grass
        In praise of their surroundings: the old man standing
Like an oracle, among birds – his arms, outstretched
        In a gesture so simple, we might mistake the dancing

He does, for an attempt at flight – a lover's humility
        Dissipating, *in* time . . . into ash, into bottles, broken
Against the crags in the creek bank; the picnic tables
        No one uses, standing alone – so solitary, so sublime

In the weight of their construction, we could believe
        Almost anything: the shy vernacular of late romance,
Where we all might live in a world of simple pleasure
        Or, eventually, supercede time – &, almost be happy.

The Beginning

An hour after the chemo begins,
my mother vomits her tea
into a plastic kidney basin.
She has the bland look
of a newborn after a wet burp,
no warning, no distress,
just, *It happens.* And there,
floating in the basin
is a cut green bean,
perfectly preserved – undisturbed
since last night's dinner. This,
the beginning of the end –
food that will not nourish,
the body's letting go,
and standing in the doorway
a doctor, whose intent look
is simply his trying to remember her name.

Bone Dream

The stone on our nightstand holds
a mountain we have climbed,
and though now we sometimes lose
by day what we gained at night,

we have come this far,
at least as far as the pebbles
we arced over a pond
wider than our arms or bodies could know,

farther than schoolchildren
could ever imagine as they dream
back and forth, swinging
on iron chains

that chirp like a lone
cricket to the everlasting moon,
earth's beautiful headstone.

Raffia

> *To the Igbo, everything is family, everything*
> *is connected, Grandmother explained.*
> *Like the weave of this raffia hat, we intertwine.*
> *See? This is the world to the Igbo.*
>   – Chris Abani

To the Igbo, everything is family, everything –
be it small or grand. Whether you look like
I do or look otherwise; whether you can sing
or have no voice at all. In all of nature – moon
fish, elephant tusks, the silkworm and its
kin – there are no essential distinctions that
can be made. Those who discriminate bring
dishonor to our house, perpetuate the shame
we never want to admit. When we're singled out,
we wilt needlessly. Relatively speaking, everyone

is connected, Grandmother explained.
We bleed the blood of both the aborigine
and the Inca. Our imagination doesn't strain
under ice-plains or inside the heat of the Gobi
or any other desert at the thought that we all
advance, slow as turtles, but we advance as one.
(And those who cannot, we must save like grains
of rice fallen from the rice-pot. When we refuse,
we are doomed to sever the connection, the link
that proclaims we are human, maintains that

like the weave of this raffia hat, we intertwine –
the lock of your blond hair braided with my
dark lock, your breathing identical to mine.)
After all, is there a line separating the clouds
covering your city and mine? Even the caesura
between twilight and nightshade cannot be
assigned with precision. All of history is a sign
that we learn and fail and fail again at the very
same rate. That I hold the tether and decide each
bend in the path your lost sheep will take. Don't you

see? This is the world to the Igbo.
To think otherwise is to dwell in double doubt.
To live otherwise is to live where there is no
point to living. This is not difficult. This won't fill
your basket with kolanut. This is a story to be
read by us all every day. We all have a grandmother
who has confirmed it, so you cannot say it isn't so.
Some young men from another tribe near your village
are waiting for your call. Their breath is indistinguishable
from yours. Welcome each one to the world of the Igbo.

Grandmother

She moved in a cloud world
down the curved staircase
into the pre-dawn hours

I had been sleeping
on a bench beside the stairs
waiting
I had been riding a white horse
for miles
under a crescent moon

She took my hand
led me to the living room
blue silk gown and matching robe,
her thin shoulders curled
slightly forward

We sat quietly
looking out at the dark
where the bones of her garden lay
The deer she whispered
I leaned in

Her long-fingered hands held mine
I saw her elegant blue veins
the morphine patches on her arms
The deer she said
a moon-colored doe stepped out
of her marrow, her pain

I saw it glow there, haloed
inside the night,
travel past the wintering garden
and enter a stand of white pine

Women and Birds

My grandmother didn't talk
much about Hitler, the camps,
or life before Milwaukee.
Quiet like a secret, she told me
Dachau had little color, the gray
sky overwhelmed with ashes of Jews.

Often the women would search the sky
for birds, search for the butterfly yellow
of wings, with eyes wide hungry
for anything able to fly.

Once she whispered to me
about the time she found
a tiny bird   dead in the snow –
how later she would finger-dig
its small grave in the frozen soil –

but not until she held the sweet
weight, the still warm body,
up to her face, breathed feathers,
and the bittersweet hope of flight.

On Aging

I am interested in the way old people kiss,
touching their lips and holding,
the same way children kiss each other,
but with less fanfare, and with a knowledge
of something lost in taking,
in giving, something bestowed.

I am learning something as years pass
about the translucency of old hands,
age showing a preference for bones,
taking gentle pleasure in revealing at last
a portion of what has been hidden.

The skin on the back of my own hands has softened
into a fine new cloth, a cloudmap,
a pattern of water seen through water;
eventually we all turn to glass,
which is the same as turning to light.

For the first time I have a friend my age who,
like a maiden aunt, instead of kissing
brushes her cheek against mine, so tender I want
to cry out, or hold my breath,
skin touching skin, taking away, leaving behind.

I remember the day, not long ago,
when my face bent under my fingertips
in a way it had never done before,
at once stiff and pliant, staying
a moment where I had put it,
each day a longer moment;
finally it will be a photograph of a face, tinted
by hand in soft, lost colors.

Someday the mark of each next kiss
will stay on my cheek forever.
When that day comes I'll be beautiful, God willing,
wearing a face that's scarred with blessings
and all the promise of the redemption
that shines from within and defies time passing.

White Woman Crossing the Delaware

Once, I played Pocahontas, danced
ancient calls of Callicoon, Tennanah Lake, Fishs Eddy
I stomped puffballs, watched smoke signals smudge the air
My sister and I hunted Indian graves
Who was buried in our forest
Whoopwhoopwhoops piercing invisible hearts
Our hands asking those who surrendered

Who   Why   How

•

Only the river raves when I visit my grandmother
A hospice angel floats by, swabs her
Such a good girl. My grandmother ungnarls her hands
I cringe from her bony grasp. From needles
that sting her like honeybees

Fear is an amulet. A cold noose of beads

•

With each moan, a window opens
Mesas of bone, flesh, torn totems

•

I wander white-washed corridors
Hospital windows gleam
look-outs to these Catskill woods
I imagine corn dances beyond the Delaware
Lenni-Lenape asleep by fires, the wings
of broken souls. Of Carolina parakeets
before a staccato of colonial guns
How memory can gather clay families,
cardboard crops, Magic Marker farms
Place them in a schoolgirl's museum
A collection of voices the birches might remember

wolf   turtle   turkey
munsee   *unami*   *unalatchitgo*

•

Night drifts toward this antiseptic port
When I close my eyes, each breath is a harbor
as I sit with an old woman who is matriarch of my tribe
Who speaks of names, of villages razed
beyond waters she can never cross again
She whispers a language comfortable as the skin I wear,
strokes my hair like a balalaika
Bubbaleh, she tells me, *I have given birth to a baby boy*
and his name is Albert, my first
Her words are ripples
mammeleh, sholem, a gute nacht

•

Delaware, I ask your aortal waters –
Can the dead hear our lullabies
in their stilled cradles
How, I ask the surrendered
will I live without grandmother
What will happen when she passes
beyond all rivers and no one is left
to witness her song

Elegy / in advance / do not hasten

1.

Caught – between the prayer for healing and the prayer
For the dead – most unappeasable and un-
Consoled remembrances – the words I need
The most, and cannot say – *hineini*, I am here,
The nowhere man, and I address no-one
Unceasingly – What meanings will be carried
Over for us now, and who will hear –
Tell me – No-One – now that, mother to son
No more remembrance is to be allowed –
And who will recognize us as we are? –
I am undone by minutes – I am undone
By days – mother – taking her hand – afraid
What to ask – doubtful what to pray –
Remembering – as she pulls her hand away –

2.

Mystery visitor of the constantly strange moment,
mother
of disappearingness,
sitting in church without her memory –

what to do with these fretful hands
but fold them together o God –
Quieting herself

among the knots and tangles, dropped threads, the clutter
of self and unself she once

would have cleared away,
and answering what half-heard voices of before
cross her face with strickenness –

household saint
who swept the room and prepared the food and served it,
then stood to one side so the men
could do their work,

humble Martha, handmaiden of the Lord
with her reticent smile, her
pale private frown –

         ∾

Sometimes we sit
and lose our memory together,
I can almost stop presuming I
am here,
each turning of time becoming
the purest other,
the questions not asked remaining where they are –

Sometimes we worry the surfaces of things,
she tears at scars and bruises on her face,
has to be taken by the hand –

Holding hands I think
I am becoming her,
as we must have been not separate once
if there was heaven,
one single fate of lostness to come, if there is not,
and what tears do I mean to drag out of her this way
with the smallest tenderness,
for my own wishing –
will I snap her out of it, since I am also Dad,
shake her and say *let's scream our little heads off,*
fly off the fucking handle together for once –

for what –
she doesn't know who I am –

&

Sometimes she mentions *her first husband*
and there was only one,
sounding like someone she maybe liked a little better –

She hums –
sits at the window for someone to arrive
and take her
home – *one of my children* –
leaving any day now,
someone else can have that room –
she hums,
as you might do if you don't have a word
or stop knowing how,
not even so you would hear
unless everything paused,
a solitary
conversation you might have no part in, a refrain,
nodding so very often to agree or remember to be there and the air
that breathes
you don't have to think about,
if you had a thought
you could let it cross your face
if somebody speaks
or sings what you would
sing, a little shine,
or was to sit by your side
with a light in his eye
that if you loved me
you wouldn't want to hasten,

or hasten,
or bid me,
or adieu –

Last seat

in a waiting room
filled with not telling

lumps of sorrow
simmering pain

once in a while
we rise to our names

still crying for angels
to rescue the future

or turn things around
with another denouement

visible signals
benevolent whispers

undamaged wings

Returning from an Evening Wake

What kind of gravity pulls a thing up?
Eight tiny frogs cling to my storm door,
attracted to the light like moths,
their igneous skin like those stones
I sometimes find by the river –
smooth, damp, barely pink,
all the fire rinsed out of them.
When I pluck one off the glass,
I feel the suck let go, a tiny
release. It flings against
the covered bridge of my hands –
a cold knock on the door that is my flesh.

To Grief

Oh other country
which we never left
rich in anniversaries
each in turn wearing your crown
how many of them are there
like stars returning every one alone
from where they have been all the time
each one the only one
and to whom do you belong
incomparable one

recurring never to be touched again
whether by hand or understanding
familiar presence suddenly approaching
already turned away
reminder hidden
in the names

back of the same sky
that lights the days as we watch them
what do you want it for
this endless longing that is only ours
orbiting even in our syllables
why do you keep calling us as you do
from the beginning without a sound
like a shadow

Grief

The cry
of the crows,
the crows of Ginsberg's "Kaddish"
caw   caw   caw...
comes closest.

We sat together in the hospital holding hands
only hours before the end

I never wanted to let you go.
You never wanted me to let you go.
Yet...

Grief can't really be approached by art
except maybe a little bit in sound

caw   caw   caw

In Dylan Thomas
you can detect it if you listen.
It's in Whitman

and maybe some of the dying scenes in Verdi operas – *Traviata* – *Forza* –

I helped you bathe,
grateful for the intimacy,
then we held hands,
we even joked
and then

caw caw caw

You can sense it in Bluegrass and other Celtic musics.
Hank Williams, with the tears in his voice,
came close
but he dressed it up too primly.
Grief's more
raw, unseemly

caw caw caw caw caw caw

Long Ships At Night Pass Whitefish Point

(after reading Linda Gregg)

alerted by light   occulting   there
then not there   there   then not
ride
a cemetery of waves
where old bones push fresh bones close to the surface

warned by light
appearing   disappearing
glide
over graveyard waves
where old memories push fresh memories close

if it were not for memories, for the ghosts
carrying the hundred clamoring moons,
I would be safe

cautioned by light
a glare
carried above the dunes and out   into the lake

slide
through coffin waters
where fresh skins push old skins   the waves

keep
saying I should not remember, but always
there is the sound of their breathing

alarmed by
light   then no light   light   then no

Isaiah Replies

A voice says, "Cry out!" And I said, "What shall I cry?" All the people are grass, their constancy is like the flowers of the field.... Surely the people are grass.
— Isaiah 40:6-7

Surely the people are grass.
Surely they're flat beneath the breath of pathological doubt.
They need. They are green tongues swallowing rain.
What would You have me say to them?
Should I lie? Should I comb them
with a black wind? What words?

The people are sick.
Sunlight pours yellow on their fragile green hair.

The people drink moon at midnight.
They bend in, checking the pond for clues to thirst.
They've learned salvation,
a stolen story.
Perhaps they want more. Perhaps
they want trumpets spilling doom.

Time shifts in an empty field, hoping to fill it.
You can rip them from dear soil;
You can lift them to your mouth.
They do not want a prophet's words.
They are ready for salvation,
the brief whistle of eternity.
They are ready to be split into song.

Las cosas olvidadas

Te acostumbras a dejar cosas olvidadas,
huellas,
indicios,
presagios
para algún posible regreso,
piedrecillas en los umbrales.
Así te enseñó tu abuelo,
siempre piedrecillas
recostadas sobre la tierra soleada.
Necesitas recordar a tus muertos
viven junto a ti y tú junto a ellos.
Los arrastras sobre la tierra ocre,
quieren caminar contigo.
No los puedes olvidar
viajan contigo al exilio,
a las ciudades donde nadie te espera.
Con ellos aprendes a conocer las voces
sin habla,
los pasos de los que te vigilan
para que no los olvides.
Te has convertido en sus silencios,
en lo que dejaron en la tierra inconclusa.

Forgotten Things

You become accustomed to leaving things behind,
traces,
signs,
omens
for a possible return,
small stones in the doorways
just as your grandfather taught you,
always small stones,
lying on the sunny earth.
You need to remember your dead,
they live next to you, and you with them.
You drag them over the ochre soil,
they want to walk with you,
you cannot forget them,
they travel into exile with you,
to the empty cities where nobody waits for you.
With them you learn to recognize voices
without words,
the steps of those watching you
so as not to forget them.
You have become their silences,
what they left behind in the unfinished earth.

Te encuentras en Praga,
Cracovia,
la aldea de Broder,
nadie te recibe.
De las casa incendiadas
quedan ahora jardínes secretos.
Tan solo los muertos te responden,
te dicen que estuvieron allí,
que dejaron las cosas olvidadas para tu regreso.
ahora tú regresas para ellos.

Y llueve mucho en esta travesía
como si el diluvio de agua quisiera irrumpir sobre tu rostro.
Has regresado no sabes por qué,
ni qué buscas,
ni de qué memorias hablas.

Eres una mariposa entre los insomnios,
caminas por donde caminó tu abuela.
Llevas su pulsera de granate
y su piel de ámbar,
la encuentras en el parque rodeada de lilas.
Está viva,
te espera.
En la invisibilidad de la tarde la encuentras,
estás amilagrada.
Regresas para encontrarla
y te parece espléndida la vida
porque te has podido reconciliar en su muerte.
Te gusta dejar cosas, perderlas,
tienes la certeza de los encuentros.

You are in Prague,
Krakow,
the villages of Broder,
nobody greets you.
Only secret gardens remain
of those burned-down houses.
Only the dead respond
telling you they were there
leaving things behind for your return.
Now you return for them.

It rains heavily on this crossing
as if this deluge wanted to burst in your face.
You have returned not knowing why,
or what you are searching for,
or what your memories invoke.

You are a butterfly among insomniacs
walking wherever your grandmother walked
with her garnet bracelet and her amber skin.
You find her in the park, surrounded by lilacs.
In the invisibility of the afternoon, you meet her,
she is alive waiting for you.
You are touched by a miracle.
You return to find her,
and life seems magnificent to you
because you are able to reconcile with death.
You love to leave things behind, to lose them,
you are certain of encounters.

Winter Twilight: Blackbirds, Starlings, Ascending

By rise of the feather, by rise of the wing.
By rise of Brewer's blackbird, red-winged
    blackbird, and starling.
By rise of short clear notes, sliding whistles,
    the buzzy, the chippy, the minor, the high.

All day we have been ordinary birds
in the ordinary day . . . gleaning
the bits of broken vine and grape, the insects,
the waste-grain, and bounty of the damp fields and ditches.

    Then some coded signal . . . of light, of temperature . . . .
    The sun drops low in the valley, mountain shadows extend.

You may be heading home from work, or deep in the daily routine,
strolling the long driveway down to the mailbox, walking the dog,
when from the corner of your eye you catch us ascending.

It's true, we surprise you with our lush, extravagant numbers,
our wide chevrons banking and twirling.
And how to name it: this ravel and twine, this coalescence
of dark bodies rivering, a thousand strong over your head
                              in eddies, ribbons, helixes, gyres.

        When one veers, we all veer, when one climbs
        we all climb – a galaxy of rapture, of old combinations
        of matter, of star, pulling together, pulling apart.

We are creation's deep pleasure, jubilation of feather, of wing
sweeping the valley from side to side. Joy for the sake of joy.

The music we make, unwieldy and strong, falls over your shoulders,
falls over your ears. Standing there, do you want to join us, to follow, to fly?

        Into the shining edges do you want to fly?

Words Alone Can Not Name It

Some things live beyond words.
There is a language only the skin knows,
poetry the eyes alone can recite,
entire conversations spun into existence
by not much more than a shrug.

Who can doubt the articulation
of outstretched arms, welcome news
the sound of feet hurrying down the hall
can bring, the eloquence of a few
simple glances, the fluent messages

the body sends even while walking?
Try naming the fragrance of spring,
what Claude Debussy's Clair de Lune
is saying, the vocabulary of mother's
cookies or the look your dog gives

just before you throw him a bone.
Who can name the parts of speech
glowing from a single candle in the dark,
the adjectives swarming around
a child's first few faltering steps,

the chatter in the little lights blinking
along the shore? How shall we learn
the alphabet of the stars, the watchwords
of robins, the story each heart tells
when it learns the lessons of separation?

Dew, Regardless

Do not ask if the dirt will hold the root,
the root, regardless, penetrates the dirt.
Do not ask if the root will pulse with water;
water will marry root and dirt
to make the anemone bloom. Do
not ask the anemone if its bloom will weep;
the bloom sings what aria it breathes
from notes of air, water, root and dirt.
Do not ask the air if it will inhale the sky;
the sky will turn light back to the sun. Do not
ask if it will shift its coat; the coat will grow
to cover green's body. Do not ask, do
not ask. The tiniest miracle and its maker don't
listen, busy as they are, under the ground,
washing their hands, spilling their gold.

The River Scrapes Against Night

Through the scrim of the tent
I map constellations, fearful
I may have missed one
of the bland white sheep
lined up for counting,
fuzzy with their own bleating fatigue.
No matter how hard I stare,
I can't find the boundaries
between river and canyon,
canyon and sky. Bats
swoop close, intimate,
alarming. Night keeps knocking
without a hint of politeness.
I'm not fooled
by steady breathing.
We are this small.
This brief.

The winner of the $1000 RUNES Award 2005

In a competition where the final judging
was done by poet **Lucille Clifton**

SANDRA COHEN MARGULIUS *of Wisconsin*
for her poem "Women and Birds"

The Runners-Up, who each received $100, were:
Annalynn Hammond *of Wisconsin for "Still Life"*
J. O'Nym *of Texas for "The Beginning"*

Poetry is a balancing between intellect and intuition, and if
one must choose between the two, one should always fall on
the side of intuition. –Lucille Clifton

The 2005 RUNES Award poems, we think, are wonderful examples of what Lucille Clifton means about the balance between intellect and intuition. Like Lucille Clifton, we were delighted with the quality of the poems submitted for the competition!

it's not nice to annoy the editors

People sometimes ask us what we have learned as editors about submitting our own work. Well, some of the things we've learned are probably well understood by most poets, but often forgotten. The truth is that RUNES receives an overwhelming number of poems and of those almost all are poems of great beauty and quality. In our case, each poem is read at least twice and the closer they come to acceptance the more they are read. A poem accepted for RUNES has probably been read ten times and those in the pile of last few chosen even more. Of course we are looking for excellence, but we must also keep in mind the theme, the variety on the theme, short and long, narrative, lyric, philosophical, and the shape of the book RUNES will become. Sometimes a poem we love and want will lose out at the last moment because it just doesn't seem to fit in the overall make-up of the book. Maybe the tone is too different, or the theme duplicates too closely.

Speaking only for ourselves, here are some of our particular no-nos. (Other editors may not feel the same.) While we do not hold any of these against the poem itself, still it is annoying and it's not nice to annoy the editors…

• SASEs are required. We like to write a note on our slips that inform poets "not this year". This is one of our ways of showing the importance to us of our poetry community. No SASE, we must then resort to emails – time consuming and impersonal. If no email and no SASE, then we can't respond. Contest entrants seem particularly likely to ignore the SASE. Maybe they think their check should be enough, but (see above).

• Checks that bounce. Of course this happens to all of us, but costs us a bank fee and often the check and fee are never redeemed.

• Tiny return envelopes – Often difficult to stuff everything in.

• Submissions that come with cardboard stiffening…

• Submissions that require a signature

• Submissions that come with postage due

All of the above require a special trip to the post office to stand in long lines.

• For contests, please clip the check to the entry. If we don't find the check we don't know it is to be a contest entry. Sometimes checks fall out a month later from who knows where. We hold each envelope up to the light before throwing it away. Good thing, because often a check is floating around in there.

• If you are including a contest and a regular submission in the same envelope, please include two SASEs. While we consider both entries equally, we do not keep them in the same pile and with some 2000 entry packets ...well you can imagine.

• If you have to withdraw a poem or poems for any reason, please do not send substitute poems. Too confusing. Hard to put together with original entry.

• Do not send revisions. Same reasons as above. If your poem is accepted, we can consider revisions, but remember we took your poem because we love it, and revisions may or may not improve it in our eyes.

• Please don't send more than 5 poems per entry. We sometimes receive packets of 20-40 poems. If you want to send more, send a second entry of up to 5 poems.

• We do not have page limits or line limits, but judge the poem on its own merits so please send us 12 pt. type so we can read it. We are reading a lot of poems, and trying to read them with respect.

• We have a reading period, which ends with a May 31st postmark. It is the postmark that matters. It doesn't matter if your cover letter is dated May 24th, if the postmark says June 1st or 12th, it is too late.

• We used to wait until the last minute to send in our own contest entries but we've changed our tune. Over 50% of RUNES entries come in the last week.

By then we are tired and overwhelmed. We have seen many wonderful poems throughout the reading period. Last minute entries are competing with enormous number of poems. We try to read everything fairly and great poems always rise to the surface but...give your poems a good chance and send them in a bit earlier.

• Be sure your name appears somewhere other than just the envelope. Information should be on every regular submission poem. Contest poems have no ID so should have a cover sheet with communication information. Somewhere your name should be typed or printed. We want to communicate with the correct name and sometimes we can't read the signature.

Okay, those are just some hints we hope you will find helpful. The bottom line remains: thank you for your wonderful work, for sending it to RUNES, for rejoicing with us when a poem is accepted, for understanding when we can't take one. The RUNES community is important to us, win, lose, or "close."

Thanks!

Lyn & Susan

Runes Award 2006

RUNES, A Review of Poetry will be sponsoring its fifth poetry competition in the spring of 2006.

The *RUNES Award 2006* will offer a $1000 prize plus publication in *RUNES, A Review of Poetry* for an original, unpublished poem on the theme of "Hearth." For the three runners-up: $100 each.

- There is an entry fee of $15 for three poems. The entry fee covers a one-year subscription to *RUNES*. Additional poems are $3 each.
- Your name should not appear on any of these poems.
- Each competition entry should include an 8.5" by 11" sheet with name, address, phone number, e-mail and title of each poem.
- Please put sufficient postage on your entry.
- Be sure to include a self-addressed stamped envelope (SASE) also with sufficient postage.

The final judge for this competition will be MARK DOTY.

Submit only in April & May of 2006. Deadline: May 31st, 2006.

All poems entered in the competition will be considered for publication in the 2006 issue.

> *It is* **NOT** *necessary to enter the competition to have your poems appear in* **RUNES,** *nor does entering the competition give any poet a better chance to have a poem accepted for publication.*

All who wish to submit poems without entering the competition are encouraged to do so. Each poem will be read and assessed on its own merit. Every contest entrant gets a copy of *RUNES 2006*, and there is a contributors' discount for extra copies. Don't forget the SASE!

The theme for the 2006 issue will be "Hearth," the same as the competition.

For complete information contact us at RunesRev@aol.com or check our web site: http://members.aol.com/Runes

Send all competition entries and all submissions to:
RUNES, A Review of Poetry
Arctos Press, P.O. Box 401, Sausalito, CA 94966 – 0401

To Our Subscribers

We'd like to thank all of you for the faith and commitment you've offered. We have no university or parent organization funding us— only you. You have helped us out, shown us that interest in independent publishing is still alive.

For our other readers, if you're not already a subscriber, we hope you will consider becoming one. Perhaps you'll even want to send a gift subscription to friends or family members who have an interest in poetry. Maybe you'll take a copy of *RUNES* to your local bookstore and ask them to order it, or you'll consider subscribing for your local library. A year's subscription is only $12 and since *RUNES* is over 160 pages, that's only about 7 cents a page – a bargain in these expensive times.

To Submit

Our reading period is April and May only of each year, so we will begin reading for "Hearth" in April of 2006. This theme will be considered metaphorically as well as literally. Reports in four months. Acquires first time rights only. Every contributor gets a free copy and and can purchase extra copies at a discounted price of $8 each.

We will consider simultaneous submissions, but please notify us promptly if a poem is accepted elsewhere. We do not accept previously published poems.

Send up to five poems **with a self-addressed stamped envelope** (required) to:

RUNES, A Review of Poetry
Arctos Press, P.O. Box 401, Sausalito, CA 94966 – 0401

Do not send your only copies. Poems will be recycled, and handwritten poems will not be accepted. The e-mail is for correspondence only. Please do not submit via e-mail. Please remember the **SASE. For complete information about submitting and for information about our annual competition The *RUNES* Award, check out our web site at: http://members.aol.com/Runes**

Subscription: $12   Single copy: $12   Sample copy: $10
Two-year subscription: $21

A to F

G to N

O to Z